W9-ABO-211

HOW TO OVERCOME LIFE'S ENDLESS TRIALS

VALUABLE LESSONS FROM THE LIFE OF JOSEPH

BRIDGE
LOGOS

Newberry, FL 32669

How to Overcome Life's Endless Trials:
Valuable Lessons from the Life of Joseph

Published by:
Bridge-Logos
Newberry, Florida 32669, USA
bridgelogos.com

ISBN 978-1-61036-158-3

Library of Congress Control Number: 2020943111

Edited by Lynn Copeland

Cover design by Brad Snow (SnowBizy.com)

Page design and layout by Genesis Group (genesis-group.net)

Printed in the United States of America

CONTENTS

INTRODUCTION

As I began writing this book on the amazing life of Joseph, I heard the phrase "trampled to death by ducks" from my pastor. It not only seems fitting for Joseph's many trials, but it so describes daily life, especially for the Christian—we enter the kingdom of God through many tribulations (Acts 14:22). While it's easy to imagine a quick demise by elephant, it's not so easy to imagine dying by duck. It would take a lot of ducks to kill us—probably by knocking us over and trampling us to death in a flurry of webbed feet and flapping wings.

But that is life's experience for most of us—one little hassle after another, suffocating us until we can hardly see the light of day.

There are unexpected bills, car problems, strained relationships, misunderstandings, nightmares, insomnia, problems with relatives, aging parents, identity theft, stress at work, difficulties with kids, endless minor health issues—such as a sty in the eye, a pulled neck muscle, cold sore on the lip, canker sore in the mouth, sore throat, pounding headache, earache, toothache—to major health problems. The dog threw up on the carpet, the sink is stopped up, the AC is out, the toast is burnt, and the cat brought a dead bird inside. You have cell phone problems, computer viruses, noisy neighbors, a leaking faucet, mold in the shower, rats chewing wiring in the garage, biting fleas, moles in the lawn, termites eating your house, aphids eating the plants, spider in the den, fly on the food, mosquito in the bedroom, cockroach in the pantry...and that's just by 9:00 a.m.

Then things really get bad.

Early in 2020, the unthinkable happened. The entire world was put on hold. A global pandemic put Hollywood, Wall Street, New York, and the rest of the world out of busyness. Like Joseph, our lives changed overnight, and it was as though we were suddenly living in some foreign land. Millions were forced to stay in their homes, away from loved ones, and our freedoms were curtailed. There were mass deaths, financial collapse, food and supply shortages, and unprecedented unemployment. Just as we had hope things were improving, then the racial tensions, riots, and looting began. For many it became almost unbearable.

It seems as though we make it through one trial, and there are more ducks in a row, waiting to suffocate us. The only way they can do that is if they get us down. And they won't be able to do that if we take a few lessons from the life of Joseph—a leaf from the world's most beloved Book. Through the Scriptures we have the consolation that the ducks of this life are not worthy to be compared to the glory that shall be ours. They work for us a far more exceeding and eternal weight of glory.

Chapter One

WHEN THINGS ARE HUMMING

"Lie with me..." The words of Potiphar's lusty wife weren't talking about bearing false witness. Her words echoed in Joseph's youthful ears. How could this be happening? This was his master's wife, and day after day she kept whispering that same seductive invitation: "Lie with me..." (Genesis 39:7).

For a young man devoid of understanding, it would be a dream come true—to hear the words, "I have spread my bed with tapestry, colored coverings of Egyptian linen. I have perfumed my bed with myrrh, aloes, and cinnamon. Come, let us take our fill of love until morning; let us delight ourselves with love. For my husband is not at home..." (Proverbs 7:16–19).

Her husband *wasn't* at home, and when Potiphar did come back she certainly wouldn't say anything. *No one would know.* But such thoughts didn't enter the mind of this Hebrew slave. Unlike the Egyptians who enslaved him, Joseph believed that there was only one God and that His omniscient eyes were in every place. He also knew that to commit adultery was to sin against Him and incur His wrath.

Joseph's conscience whispered,

> Do not let your heart turn aside to her ways,
> Do not stray into her paths;
> For she has cast down many wounded,
> And all who were slain by her were strong men.
> Her house is the way to hell,
> Descending to the chambers of death. (Proverbs 7:25–27)

Yet, the temptress kept tempting him relentlessly, day after day. He was a slave and dared not run away. That was a dead end. One alternative was to be upfront with his master, but what could he say: "Your wife is a whorish woman"? That wouldn't fly. No matter how he tried to cut it, it sounded bad. Bad for Joseph. His master wouldn't believe the word of a slave over the word of his beloved wife.

Most of us battle temptations to sin. The world, the flesh, and the devil whisper of its delights.

Besides, this wouldn't just be a matter of committing adultery. It was more than that. Three times in Genesis 39 Scripture reiterates that Joseph had been trusted with *all* that Potiphar had. *Everything.* Presumably he handled the general finances, staff wages, taxes, upkeep of the buildings, laying out his master's clothes, ordering food for family and staff, organizing the household cleaning, including camel and horse health, chariot maintenance, etc. Joseph had been entrusted with everything; he was allowed access to everything except his master's beloved wife. How then could he do this great wickedness, and sin against God (Genesis 39:9)? Those are the very words Joseph used to try to deter this loose woman. He was appealing to her conscience. This wouldn't be right! But she had no conscience, no love of righteousness, no fear of God, and also evidently no love for her husband.

Most of us battle temptations to sin. The world, the flesh, and the devil whisper of its delights. We continually fight the lust of the eyes, the lust of the flesh, and the pride of life. But how can we give ourselves to sin—in light of everything we have in Christ? God gave us life, knowledge of what is right and wrong, forgiveness through the cross, and the precious gospel with which we've been entrusted. Like Joseph, we say, "How then can I do this great wickedness, and sin against God?"

Joseph was between a rock and a hard place. The ducks were coming, and they were starting to suffocate him.

Life in Egypt had been going so well, but how complicated this woman was now making it. He thought back to the simplicity of his younger days, and how he'd suddenly been thrown a curveball...

Joseph was just seventeen. He was strikingly handsome, young, and vibrant. His entire life stood before him. He had no financial woes—he had a secure job, with the big plus that his father was wealthy and favored him. His life entailed that of a carefree farmhand, tending to his father's sheep. Things were humming for young Joseph.

Perhaps the most dangerous time for us as Christians is when things are humming. There's money in the bank and the family is happy, healthy, wealthy, and wise. That's when we can think that we need not pray or search God's Word. That's when we can think that minute-by-minute trust isn't needed. And that thought should frighten us.

We tend to pray most in a storm. Peace doesn't normally produce passionate prayer. Having the ability to keep control of our lives rarely drives us to our knees. Why should it? Yet our humble knees are our special place of safety.

Still, we naturally long for prosperous and storm-free times. Who doesn't like to be able to pay the rent, buy food and clothing for the family, and now and then help others who are struggling? There's nothing wrong with peace and prosperity, but when they cause us to drift from God, the blessing becomes a curse.

Storms tend to anchor us in God. And so He, in His great love and infinite wisdom, often sends them to those He loves to bring us to the shelter of the harbor.

The way to navigate through all the incoming ducks is to understand the story Jesus gave of the wise and foolish house builders. It's also important to know the context of the story by reading the preceding three verses:

> "Not everyone who says to Me, 'Lord, Lord,' shall enter the kingdom of heaven, but he who does the will of My Father in heaven. Many will say to Me in that day, 'Lord, Lord, have we not prophesied in Your name, cast out demons in Your name, and done many wonders in Your name?' And then I will declare to them, 'I never knew you; depart from Me, you who practice lawlessness!'" (Matthew 7:21–23)

There will be many on the Day of Judgment who profess to be Christians and will find that they are not, as evidenced by their lawlessness. Then comes the warning from Jesus about the two house builders, beginning with "therefore" to give context:

> "Therefore whoever hears these sayings of Mine, and does them, I will liken him to a wise man who built his house on the rock: and the rain descended, the floods came, and the winds blew and beat on that house; and it did not fall, for it was founded on the rock. But everyone who hears these sayings of Mine, and does not do them, will be like a foolish man who built his house on the sand: and the rain descended, the floods came, and the winds blew and beat

on that house; and it fell. And great was its fall." (verses 24–27)

The "many" are those who hear the sayings of Jesus and don't do them. This includes not only the godless world that ignores the gospel warning, but the many who sit in churches —those who are hearers only, and not doers of the Word (James 1:22).

Both house builders encountered the same storms. They are inevitable. We would be wise, therefore, to check our foundation before they arrive.

So before we look closely at the fascinating life of Joseph and his suffocating ducks, let's ask the question, "Is my life built on the teachings of Jesus?" Scripture says to examine ourselves and see if we're in the faith (2 Corinthians 13:5). Here is a checklist of ten questions to see if we've passed from death to life, keeping in mind that we don't do these things *to* be saved, but *because* we're saved:

Storms are inevitable. We would be wise, therefore, to check our foundation before they arrive.

1. Am I sharing the gospel with the unsaved (Mark 16:15)?

2. Am I reading God's Word daily?

3. Do I have a heart that longs to do God's will?

4. Am I bridling my appetites?

5. Am I in regular fellowship?

6. Is God, rather than money, my source of joy and provider of peace for the future?

7. Do I keep my word?

8. Am I confessing and forsaking all sin?

9. Do I have a loving and forgiving attitude toward others?

10. Do I see times of prosperity to be times of danger?

THE NARRATIVE BEGINS

Our story of Joseph begins to unfold in Genesis 37:

> Now Jacob dwelt in the land where his father was a stranger, in the land of Canaan. This is the history of Jacob. Joseph, being seventeen years old, was feeding the flock with his brothers. (verses 1,2)

In Luke 24, after Jesus had risen from the dead, He joined in a conversation between two of His disciples on the road to a village called Emmaus, which was about seven miles from Jerusalem. He asked them what they were discussing, and they replied that the chief priests and rulers handed Jesus over to be crucified, and it was the third day since it took place. Then they said,

> Yes, and certain women of our company, who arrived at the tomb early, astonished us. When they did not find His body, they came saying that they had also seen a vision of angels who said He was alive. (Luke 24:22–24)

After Jesus firmly rebuked them for their lack of faith, the Scriptures say,

> And beginning at Moses and all the Prophets, He expounded to them in all the Scriptures the things concerning Himself. (verse 27)

His referral to "Moses" was a reference to the books that Moses penned, which included the story of Joseph. Perhaps Jesus, during this conversation, pointed out the parallels and types between His life and the life of Joseph. As we will see in the following pages, there were many. One of them was that Joseph was a shepherd who tended his father's flock.

In John chapter 10 Jesus is portrayed as the Great Shepherd who tended His Father's flock. He spoke of an intimate relationship between Himself and those who follow Him, knowing each of us by name (John 10:2,3).

While the world looks down its proud nose because the Bible likens believers to sheep (atheists mockingly call us "sheeple"), there are only two categories of people. We are either easily led sheep, or applicably stubborn and rebellious goats.

Yet in speaking of the lost state of humanity, Isaiah likens *all* of mankind to sheep:

> All we like sheep have gone astray;
> We have turned, every one, to his own way;
> And the Lord has laid on Him the iniquity of us all.
> (Isaiah 53:6)

There is a sense of safety in a flock of sheep. The shepherd can keep his protective eye on the flock. But when one sheep turns to its own way and goes astray, it becomes easy pickings for a predator with a taste for tenderloin.

As sheep, Christians are willingly led because our soul pants after the Good Shepherd. We are sheep who have been rescued from the mouth of the lion. We were once lost, but now we are found. Jesus left the ninety-nine to seek and save us, and He now leads us by the still waters and into green pastures:

> And when he brings out his own sheep, he goes before them; and the sheep follow him, for they know his voice.
> (John 10:4)

Things were sweet for young Joseph. But something was about to happen to make things sour. The first of many ducks was getting ready to show its ugly head.

Questions

1. Name several things that Potiphar's wife lacked.

2. Is it true for you that we pray most in a storm? Share an experience.

3. Have the storms of life weakened you or made you stronger? What is it that determines whether we are strengthened or weakened?

4. How will it help us in trials if we believe that they come by God's permissive will? Give some biblical examples.

5. How are Christians like sheep and the unsaved like goats?

Chapter Two

THE EVIL REPORT

Trouble started for Joseph as he was tending the flock with his brothers:

> And the lad was with the sons of Bilhah and the sons of Zilpah, his father's wives; and Joseph brought a bad report of them to his father. (Genesis 37:2)

We are not told what it was that the sons of Bilhah and Zilpah did, but only that what they did was bad and that Joseph told his father. Being a tattletale didn't exactly put him in his siblings' good books.

There was something else that didn't help the situation:

> Now Israel loved Joseph more than all his children, because he was the son of his old age. Also he made him a tunic of many colors. (verses 3,4)

Sometimes an afterthought-child can give a new lease on life to aging parents. Everyday pleasures, taken for granted by the young, are but fading memories to the elderly. When our children grow up, they pass us in knowledge like a motorbike in the carpool lane. They no longer give us the pleasure of sitting at our feet and learning life's lessons.

Bible scholars estimate that Jacob (Israel) was a ripe old ninety-one years of age when Joseph was born. They calculated his age by subtracting from his time of meeting Pharaoh, when he was an even riper one hundred and thirty years old (see Genesis 47:9), a mere whippersnapper in Bible years. And Joseph brought pleasure back to his aging dad:

> But when his brothers saw that their father loved him more than all his brothers, they hated him and could not speak peaceably to him. (Genesis 37:4)

Jacob loved Joseph more than all his children, and as a token of his affection he gave his beloved son a special coat. Jesus said of His Father's love:

> "The Father loves the Son, and has given all things into His hand." (John 3:35)

> "Therefore My Father loves Me, because I lay down My life that I may take it again." (John 10:17)

God the Father so loved the Son that He once broke through the heavens and said, "This is My beloved Son, in whom I am well pleased" (Matthew 3:17). That could be said of no other human being. Jesus alone pleased the Father when every other human being justly angered Him because of their sin (see John 3:36). In our sinful state, we could never please God, but Jesus did. Always:

> "And He who sent Me is with Me. The Father has not left Me alone, *for I always do those things that please Him.*" (John 8:29, emphasis added)

Jesus was different. He was clothed in perfect righteousness, given to Him by His Father:

I will greatly rejoice in the Lord,
My soul shall be joyful in my God;
For He has clothed me with the garments of salvation,
He has covered me with the robe of righteousness,
As a bridegroom decks himself with ornaments,
And as a bride adorns herself with her jewels. (Isaiah 61:10)

However, when Joseph's brothers saw that their father loved him more than all of them, they hated him.

Beware of the tiniest spark of jealousy. It is the subtlest of sins, because it starts as a mere ember in the tinder-dry heart. It is dangerous because it is fueled by pride, envy, a festering anger, and a blinding hatred that often leads to the inferno of murder.

Jealousy is the subtlest of sins, because it starts as a mere ember in the tinder-dry heart.

Joseph's brothers hated him because their father didn't see the danger of filial favoritism. In his commentary, Matthew Henry stated,

But Jacob made known his love, by dressing Joseph finer than the rest of his children. It is wrong for parents to make a difference between one child and another, unless there is great cause for it, by the children's dutifulness, or undutifulness. When parents make a difference, children soon notice it, and it leads to quarrels in families.

Joseph's brothers "*could not* speak peaceably to him." Their hatred wouldn't allow them to give him the courtesy of a peaceful word. That's because when we give ourselves to sin, we become servants of sin. In John 8:34, Jesus warned,

"Most assuredly, I say to you, whoever commits sin is a slave of sin."

In humanity's very first siblings, we see Cain didn't listen to God's warning about its power:

> And in the process of time it came to pass that Cain brought an offering of the fruit of the ground to the LORD. Abel also brought of the firstborn of his flock and of their fat. And the LORD respected Abel and his offering, but He did not respect Cain and his offering. And Cain was very angry, and his countenance fell.
>
> So the LORD said to Cain, "Why are you angry? And why has your countenance fallen? If you do well, will you not be accepted? And if you do not do well, sin lies at the door. And its desire is for you, but you should rule over it." (Genesis 4:3–7)

When Cain harbored jealousy and anger in his heart that was festering into hatred, God told him that sin lay at the door, and that he was not to allow it to rule over him. He took no notice of the divine warning, opened the door wide, and murdered his own brother:

> For this is the message that you heard from the beginning, that we should love one another, not as Cain who was of the wicked one and murdered his brother. And why did he murder him? Because his works were evil and his brother's righteous. (1 John 3:11,12)

If we are a slave of sin, we do its bidding. We are taken captive to do its will (see 2 Timothy 2:26). Think of individuals who are guilty of domestic violence against those they profess to love. Or think of the NFL player who punches out another player in a fit of anger while being fully aware that he's being filmed from multiple angles. He knows that what he is doing is going to be aired in slow motion a hundred times by the media, cost him huge fines, and may even cost him his beloved career. But he can't control himself. Or consider those who end up murdering a stranger because of blinding road rage. Sin blinds to its consequences.

Joseph's brothers were blinded by sin. They were jealous and envious, and they hated him.

The New Testament says of Jesus that "the chief priests had handed Him over because of envy" (Mark 15:10). As Jesus said, "They hated Me without a cause" (John 15:25).

THE CRACKED DAM

Scripture was written for our learning, and our lesson here is that human nature is a cracked dam. It needs only a little pressure to weaken it and cause irreparable disaster. Joseph's brothers already hated him because he was the favored son. But something was about to happen that would bring more pressure and burst the dam:

> Now Joseph had a dream, and he told it to his brothers; and they hated him even more. So he said to them, "Please hear this dream which I have dreamed...And his brothers said to him, "Shall you indeed reign over us? Or shall you indeed have dominion over us?" So they hated him even more for his dreams and for his words. (Genesis 37:5–8)

Hatred is a deep well. His brothers already hated him, but when he told them of his dreams, they were able to hate him even more. As with Cain, their hatred then festered into a desire to murder their own brother.

Here is what brought his brothers to this murderous point:

1. Giving a bad report

Those in the world hate us because we give a bad report of their behavior. We tell them that God sees their secret sins, and He will bring them to judgment on the Day of Wrath. Jesus said that we shouldn't be surprised by their hatred. We, like Joseph, are hated—not just because we wear a robe of righteousness, or because we refuse to join them in their sin, but because we give a bad report about them. The Amplified Bible puts it this way:

> In [connection with] all this, they [the unbelievers] are resentful and surprised that you do not [think like them, value their values and] run [hand in hand] with them into the same excesses of dissipation and immoral freedom, and they criticize and abuse and ridicule you and make fun of your values. (1 Peter 4:4, AMP)

While the world sees a measure of good in everyone (never so manifest as at funerals), it seems to them that we see only sin. We are guilty of what they call "hate speech." And so we are accused of hating homosexuals, brainwashing children, hindering women's rights, and ignorantly restricting the advancement of science.

Our obligation as Christians is to speak the truth in love even if it brings the scowl of the world.

But what can we say? We know that God's testimony is true. The human heart *is* desperately wicked (Jeremiah 17:9). The daily news is proof of that. No one is good. And our obligation as Christians is to speak the truth in love even if it brings the scowl of the world. The Scriptures remind us,

> Yes, and all who desire to live godly in Christ Jesus will suffer persecution. (2 Timothy 3:12)

> "If the world hates you, you know that it hated Me before it hated you. If you were of the world, the world would love its own. Yet because you are not of the world, but I chose you out of the world, therefore the world hates you. Remember the word that I said to you, 'A servant is not

greater than his master.' If they persecuted Me, they will also persecute you. If they kept My word, they will keep yours also. But all these things they will do to you for My name's sake, because they do not know Him who sent Me. If I had not come and spoken to them, they would have no sin, but now they have no excuse for their sin. He who hates Me hates My Father also. If I had not done among them the works which no one else did, they would have no sin; but now they have seen and also hated both Me and My Father. But this happened that the word might be fulfilled which is written in their law, 'They hated Me without a cause.'" (John 15:18–25)

2. Being favored by his father

The world doesn't understand that the favor extended to us in Christ is *unmerited,* and more often than not we are accused and reviled for what they think is a condescending self-righteousness. Yet God loves us, not because we deserve His love, but because He is loving and kind by nature.

3. Receiving a robe of righteousness

We have a new heart that thirsts after righteousness. We no longer join in with their sin, and our holiness (our separation from sin) angers the world. The criminal has become a police officer and is labeled as a traitor.

4. Speaking openly of dreams

We speak openly of God and the reality of Heaven. Our soul makes its boast in the Lord. The humble hear and are glad, but the proud tell us not to be so heavenly minded that we are no earthly use. In their eyes we are deluded and are not grounded in reality. We see Him who is invisible and dream of the coming kingdom.

Questions

1. Do you think Jacob was at fault for openly favoring Joseph? Or do you think the brothers were at fault? Have you ever been guilty of favoritism?

2. Have you ever felt jealous of someone you considered more favored by God than yourself? Did jealous thoughts keep coming back to you? What do you think was their source?

3. If you did feel jealous, how did it affect your relationship with the person you were jealous of? Did you feel resentment or hatred? Did it affect your walk with the Lord?

4. Have you ever felt "road rage" (even slightly)? What happened? Did you feel justified?

5. Have you ever felt enslaved by a particular sin? How did (or do) you deal with it?

Chapter Three

THE COAT OF MANY COLORS

As we have seen, Joseph gave a bad report of his siblings. Jesus likewise gave a bad report about His Jewish brethren: "He came to His own, and His own did not receive Him" (John 1:11). He rightly called them hypocrites and white-washed tombs, and said, "Serpents, brood of vipers! How can you escape the condemnation of hell?" (Matthew 23:33).

Charles Spurgeon said of His words:

> How very faithful was our Master! He was very tender in spirit; but still, He spoke very severely. The old proverb says that "a good surgeon often cuts deeply," and so it was with the Lord Jesus Christ. He did not film the evil matter over, He lanced the wound. He is not the most loving who speaks the smoothest words; true love often compels an honest man to say that which pains him far more than it affects his callous hearers... This is Christ's utterance, let me remind you. Our modern preachers would not talk like this, even to scribes and Pharisees who were crucifying Christ afresh, and putting Him to an open flame. They

would search the dictionary through to find very smooth and pretty words to say to Christ's enemies. We are not of their way of thinking and speaking, nor shall we be while we desire to follow in the footsteps of our Lord.

The religious leaders hated Jesus for such cutting words. And that hatred quickly led to attempted murder. After His first public sermon, they tried to kill Him by throwing Him off a cliff:

> [They] rose up and thrust Him out of the city; and they led Him to the brow of the hill on which their city was built, that they might throw Him down over the cliff. (Luke 4:29)

They also said that Jesus was insane:

Such a thought would have been further fuel for his brothers' uncontrollable robe rage.

> Then the multitude came together again, so that they could not so much as eat bread. But when His own people heard about this, they went out to lay hold of Him, for they said, "He is out of His mind." (Mark 3:20,21)

As with Joseph and his dreams, Jesus also spoke of His future glory:

> "Hereafter you will see the Son of Man sitting at the right hand of the Power, and coming on the clouds of heaven." (Matthew 26:64)

Scripture tells us of Joseph's brothers:

> Now when they saw him afar off, even before he came near them, they conspired against him to kill him. Then they said to one another, "Look, this dreamer is coming! Come therefore, let us now kill him and cast him into some pit; and we shall say, 'Some wild beast has devoured

him.' We shall see what will become of his dreams!'"
(Genesis 37:18–20)

They no doubt saw him from afar, even before he came
near them, because of his coat of many colors, just as the
religious leaders saw Jesus afar off because of His robe of
perfect righteousness. They stood back in their condescen-
sion and hated the light. His love of the poor, fellowship with
sinners, His cleansing of the temple, fiery rebukes, and
refusal to bow to their man-centered traditions infuriated
them.

Some believe that Joseph's robe was more than a mere
fashion statement, but that it was symbolic that he was Jacob's
heir:

> It marked the owner as the one whom the father intended
> to be the future leader of the household, an honor nor-
> mally given to the firstborn son.[1]

Such a thought would have been further fuel for his
brothers' uncontrollable robe rage.

In Matthew 21 Jesus spoke a parable to the religious leaders. He said,

> "Hear another parable: There was a certain landowner
> who planted a vineyard and set a hedge around it, dug a
> winepress in it and built a tower. And he leased it to vine-
> dressers and went into a far country. Now when vintage-
> time drew near, he sent his servants to the vinedressers,
> that they might receive its fruit. And the vinedressers took
> his servants, beat one, killed one, and stoned another.
> Again he sent other servants, more than the first, and they
> did likewise to them. Then last of all he sent his son to
> them, saying, 'They will respect my son.' But when the
> vinedressers saw the son, they said among themselves,
> 'This is the heir. Come, let us kill him and seize his inheri-

tance.' So they took him and cast him out of the vineyard and killed him." (Matthew 21:33–39)

TAMAR'S ROBE OF MANY COLORS

In 2 Samuel 13 we read that after Amnon raped his sister Tamar, he hated her:

> Then Amnon hated her exceedingly, so that the hatred with which he hated her was greater than the love with which he had loved her. And Amnon said to her, "Arise, be gone!"
>
> So she said to him, "No, indeed! This evil of sending me away is worse than the other that you did to me."
>
> But he would not listen to her. Then he called his servant who attended him, and said, "Here! Put this woman out, away from me, and bolt the door behind her." Now she had on a robe of many colors, for the king's virgin daughters wore such apparel. And his servant put her out and bolted the door behind her. (2 Samuel 13:15–18)

Amnon's failure to control his lustful appetites let the enemy come in, steal his love, and replace it with hatred:

> Whoever has no rule over his own spirit is like a city broken down, without walls. (Proverbs 25:28)

Tamar's robe of many colors set her apart as a pure virgin. Joseph was set apart by Jacob as being a special son, and Jesus was set apart by the Father as the only begotten Son, a pure and spotless Lamb.

Questions

1. Why did the Jewish leaders hate Jesus? Have you ever been hated for your faith? Share an experience.

2. Have you ever had a dream in which you thought God was speaking to you? Are you embarrassed to tell others of the dream? If so, why?

3. Has the world ever mocked you as being a "dreamer"? Give the details.

4. The Scriptures tell us that Amnon "loved" Tamar. What happened to that love? How can love be reconciled by his actions?

5. What can we learn from Amnon?

Chapter Four

MORE BROTHERLY FUEL

We learn to walk by bruising. A toddler falls seven times and rises eight. And we learn to talk in a similar way. Words can have bruising consequences. How many of us have looked at the Book of James about how our tongue can start a fire, and through experience obeyed "let every man be swift to hear, slow to speak" (James 1:19)? I'm sure Joseph often pondered the wisdom of his youthful talk about his dreams.

> Then he dreamed still another dream and told it to his brothers, and said, "Look, I have dreamed another dream. And this time, the sun, the moon, and the eleven stars bowed down to me." So he told it to his father and his brothers; and his father rebuked him and said to him, "What is this dream that you have dreamed? Shall your mother and I and your brothers indeed come to bow down to the earth before you?" And his brothers envied him, but his father kept the matter in mind. (Genesis 37:9–11)

Jacob rebuked Joseph for such foolish talk. But it seems that he later reconsidered that what he said was out of character. While Joseph's dreams stirred envy and jealousy in his brothers, his father *kept the matter in mind*—like Mary did when shepherds spoke of their hard-to-believe experience of being approached by an angelic host:

> And they came with haste and found Mary and Joseph, and the Babe lying in a manger. Now when they had seen Him, they made widely known the saying which was told them concerning this Child. And all those who heard it marveled at those things which were told them by the shepherds. But Mary kept all these things and pondered them in her heart. (Luke 2:16–19)

Like Joseph, Mary didn't consider the shepherds' statements to be idle dreams.

A dozen years later, the Scriptures say a similar thing of her regarding Jesus. After Mary and Joseph accidentally left him in Jerusalem, they returned looking for the twelve-year-old Jesus. Luke tells us:

> Now so it was that after three days they found Him in the temple, sitting in the midst of the teachers, both listening to them and asking them questions. And all who heard Him were astonished at His understanding and answers. So when they saw Him, they were amazed; and His mother said to Him, "Son, why have You done this to us? Look, Your father and I have sought You anxiously."
>
> And He said to them, "Why did you seek Me? Did you not know that I must be about My Father's business?" But they did not understand the statement which He spoke to them.
>
> Then He went down with them and came to Nazareth, and was subject to them, but His mother kept all these things in her heart. (Luke 2:46–51)

What Jesus said made no sense to them, but His mother knew that He was special and "kept all these things in her heart." Jacob did the same with Joseph and his peculiar dreams.

> Then his brothers went to feed their father's flock in Shechem. And Israel said to Joseph, "Are not your brothers feeding the flock in Shechem? Come, I will send you to them."
>
> So he said to him, "Here I am."
>
> Then he said to him, "Please go and see if it is well with your brothers and well with the flocks, and bring back word to me." So he sent him out of the Valley of Hebron, and he went to Shechem. (Genesis 37:12–14)

Joseph's evil report of his brothers had revealed a betrayal of trust between them and their father. We don't know the specifics of the evil in which they were involved. Perhaps they stole sheep, or sold some of their father's flock to passing travelers and divided the money between themselves. Whatever the case, Jacob asked Joseph for a report of the well-being of both his sons and his flocks. He said, "Bring back word to me."

Joseph's evil report of his brothers had revealed a betrayal of trust between them and their father.

> Now a certain man found him, and there he was, wandering in the field. And the man asked him, saying, "What are you seeking?"
>
> So he said, "I am seeking my brothers. Please tell me where they are feeding their flocks."
>
> And the man said, "They have departed from here, for I heard them say, 'Let us go to Dothan.'" So Joseph went after his brothers and found them in Dothan. (Genesis 37:15–17)

This "certain man" guided Joseph to his brothers. That one seemingly insignificant experience was a huge part of

God's permissive will for the life of Joseph. God could have directed Joseph Himself, but He chose a human vessel to direct him. This is often the way with God. Jesus told His disciples to look for a "certain man" who was carrying a vessel of water to guide them to where Jesus would have His last Passover before the cross:

> And He said, "Go into the city to a certain man, and say to him, 'The Teacher says, "My time is at hand; I will keep the Passover at your house with My disciples."'" (Matthew 26:18)

Sometimes God uses certain people to guide us into His will. Often we don't see His hand until after the fact. But when we look back we see amazing divine repercussions—all because of the words or actions of one seemingly insignificant "certain man."

While I was ministering in Hawaii back in the late 1980s, a certain man introduced me to a pastor from California. The pastor sat in on the teachings, called me some months later in New Zealand, and invited us to move our ministry to the United States. Some years later our television show was birthed, which has aired for years in 190 countries and been used by God to touch countless lives. Our three kids grew up in the United States, married wonderful Americans, and that birthed nine grandchildren. All because of a "certain man."

And this unnamed man directed Joseph to his brothers:

> Now when they saw him afar off, even before he came near them, they conspired against him to kill him. Then they said to one another, "Look, this dreamer is coming! Come therefore, let us now kill him and cast him into some pit; and we shall say, 'Some wild beast has devoured him.' We shall see what will become of his dreams!"
>
> But Reuben heard it, and he delivered him out of their hands, and said, "Let us not kill him." And Reuben said to

them, "Shed no blood, but cast him into this pit which is in the wilderness, and do not lay a hand on him"—that he might deliver him out of their hands, and bring him back to his father.

So it came to pass, when Joseph had come to his brothers, that they stripped Joseph of his tunic, the tunic of many colors that was on him. Then they took him and cast him into a pit. And the pit was empty; there was no water in it. (Genesis 37:18–24)

It is said that blood is thicker than water. In other words, love is deeper and bonds are stronger within families. But this wasn't the case in the face of the monster of jealousy. It devoured what family love there was and replaced it with murderous intent. They *delighted* at the thought of shedding their own brother's blood.

Joseph was rejected by his brethren and condemned to death. Jesus too was despised and rejected:

Who has believed our report?
And to whom has the arm of the Lord been revealed?
For He shall grow up before Him as a tender plant,
And as a root out of dry ground.
He has no form or comeliness;
And when we see Him,
There is no beauty that we should desire Him.
He is despised and rejected by men,
A Man of sorrows and acquainted with grief.
And we hid, as it were, our faces from Him;
He was despised, and we did not esteem Him. (Isaiah 53:1–3)

Jesus' own brethren called for His death because they so hated Him:

"We will not have this man to reign over us." (Luke 19:14)

But they shouted, saying, "Crucify Him, crucify Him!" (Luke 23:21)

Joseph's brothers were so callous that they ignored his anguished cries for mercy and sat down to enjoy themselves:

> And they sat down to eat a meal. Then they lifted their eyes and looked, and there was a company of Ishmaelites, coming from Gilead with their camels, bearing spices, balm, and myrrh, on their way to carry them down to Egypt. So Judah said to his brothers, "What profit is there if we kill our brother and conceal his blood? Come and let us sell him to the Ishmaelites, and let not our hand be upon him, for he is our brother and our flesh." And his brothers listened. (Genesis 37:25–27)

With murder off the table, they sat down to eat a meal, before Judah persuaded them to sell Joseph into slavery.

Joseph's brothers were so callous that they ignored his anguished cries for mercy and sat down to enjoy themselves.

> Then Midianite traders passed by; so the brothers pulled Joseph up and lifted him out of the pit, and sold him to the Ishmaelites for twenty shekels of silver. And they took Joseph to Egypt.
>
> Then Reuben returned to the pit, and indeed Joseph was not in the pit; and he tore his clothes. And he returned to his brothers and said, "The lad is no more; and I, where shall I go?"
>
> So they took Joseph's tunic, killed a kid of the goats, and dipped the tunic in the blood. Then they sent the tunic of many colors, and they brought it to their father and said, "We have found this. Do you know whether it is your son's tunic or not?"
>
> And he recognized it and said, "It is my son's tunic. A wild beast has devoured him. Without doubt Joseph is torn to pieces." (Genesis 37:28–33)

Joseph was stripped of his coat of many colors. Pastor Geoff Thomas writes of Jesus:

The New Testament pays some attention to the clothes that Jesus wore at each stage of his life. At his birth he was wrapped in swaddling clothes in the stable. It was all a sign of his humiliation; he was put down to sleep in one of the mangers into which the hay was thrown for animal fodder. The place where the little Lord Jesus lay down his sweet head was raised up off the floor—safe from the attack of rats while Mary and Joseph slept in the darkness. Seeing him in his swaddling bands, and lying in that feeding trough, other humble people—the shepherds—received the sign that a Saviour had come who was suitable for them, the very one who'd been announced to them by the angel.

Then throughout Jesus' ministry there was nothing that distinguished the clothes he wore from anybody else. John the Baptist wore a very severe garb, but Jesus' clothes were like everyone else's, attire suitable for weddings, other garments for sleeping, and clothes for walking long distances. During the day a Jew would wear five articles of clothing—the inner robe, the outer cloak, the sandals, the girdle or wide belt, and a turban, and that was what the Saviour would have worn—though in the pictures of him which artists have drawn they rarely portray him as wearing anything on his head. The soldiers had already crowned him with thorns.

Then on the Mount of Transfiguration Jesus' "clothes became dazzlingly white, whiter than anyone in the world could bleach them" (Mark 9:3). The glory that was his as the only begotten of the Father, full of grace and truth, burst forth, and this phenomenal transformation affected the very clothes he'd put on. His glory shone through the form that he'd taken in incarnation.[2]

Scripture says of Jesus:

And they stripped Him... (Matthew 27:28)

And when they crucified Him, they divided His garments, casting lots for them to determine what every man should take. (Mark 15:24)

Joseph's brethren sold him into slavery for silver and delivered him into the hands of the Gentiles.

Jesus was sold for silver and delivered into the hands of the Gentiles:

"What are you willing to give me if I deliver Him to you?" And they counted out to him thirty pieces of silver. (Matthew 26:15)

In Zechariah 11:12,13, thirty pieces of silver was the price Zechariah received for his labor. He took the coins and threw them "to the potter." In Exodus 21:32, thirty pieces of silver was the price of a slave.

BATTLING JEALOUSY

When the Bible says that "jealousy is a husband's fury," the context is speaking of a husband who was enraged that somebody committed adultery with his wife. Scripture says he will not spare in the day of vengeance. There is a reason for this. Jealousy is blinding. A jealous man will commit murder—killing both the offending male and even his wife.

Blinding jealousy is also the bedfellow of covetousness, greed, and selfishness. The way to fight it is to "learn" (as Paul said) to be content with what you have, and pray for God's blessing upon those you are tempted to be jealous of. It is harder to hold onto animosity when you are genuinely doing this.

We are commanded to love even our enemies, and we should therefore never be jealous of any other human being, because that is not an expression of love. Consider what Scripture says about Cain's jealousy:

> For this is the message that you heard from the beginning, that we should love one another, not as Cain who was of the wicked one and murdered his brother. (1 John 3:11,12)

Jesus spoke of jealousy in a parable about certain laborers (see Matthew 20:1–16). When some were discontent because the same wage was paid to those who didn't work through the heat of the day, Jesus told them to mind their own business (to paraphrase). And that's how we should be when jealousy seeks to find entrance into our heart. We should shut that door and lock it, because what other people do (or have) should be none of our business—if we are walking in love.

But if we make it our business, we shouldn't then be surprised when we end up with a hardened conscience, bankrupt of character—just like Joseph's jealous brothers.

God has set moral boundaries for us because He loves us. If we step over them, we do so at our own peril. Scripture warns us:

> Be sober, be vigilant; because your adversary the devil walks about like a roaring lion, seeking whom he may devour. Resist him, steadfast in the faith... (1 Peter 5:8,9)

Notice the words "he *may* devour." If you are in his territory, he has permission to devour you, and jealousy certainly gives place to the devil.

UP CLOSE AND PERSONAL

I put reflective glass on the outside of one of our large living room windows and built a bird aviary on the outside of the window. We then put in some colorful birds, and because of the mirrored glass we can get up close and personal. The birds don't know that we are looking at them. We also added a ledge and seed on the *outside* of the cage, so that wild birds could come and go. I have often wondered if the caged birds wish they could be as free as the wild birds.

One day I was horrified to see a hawk swoop in, grab one of the wild birds, and peck it to death as it screeched in terror. It was a horrible sound. I ran outside and all I found was a gruesome pool of blood. The hawk flew off with it in its claws.

I now wonder if the birds in the caged environment (that heard the awful sounds of the terrified bird) now see it as a place of safety.

Such is the way of a Christian home. Teenagers can sometimes feel trapped by boundaries given to them by their parents. What many don't realize is that the hawks are waiting. As the teens mature and look back at life in the secular world, they will see the gruesome consequences of abortion, rape, jealousy, hatred, sexually transmitted diseases, alcoholism, drug addiction, and even suicide, and thank God for the protective cage of godly boundaries.

Questions

1. Has there been a "certain" person who, in retrospect, you realized God used to direct your life?

2. Have you ever been rejected for your faith? How did it make you feel, and what was your consolation?

3. Have you ever shown love in return for hatred? Give the details. How did that make you feel?

4. Did you stray as a teenager? Are you ashamed of your sinful past, or are you tempted to boast about it?

5. What advice would you give to someone who is approaching their teenage years?

Chapter Five

A MOURNING PERSON

I often stand in awe of the police officer who has to deliver the news of the sudden death of a loved one. I don't know how they do it. I would avoid such a task like the plague. I would social-distance myself from that part of the job. Joseph's deceitful brothers didn't deliver bad news. They left their father to come to his own conclusion, by giving him Joseph's blood-drenched coat. Its many colors were now a darkened red and brought the terrible news of what seemed like his sure death.

> Then Jacob tore his clothes, put sackcloth on his waist, and mourned for his son many days. And all his sons and all his daughters arose to comfort him; but he refused to be comforted, and he said, "For I shall go down into the grave to my son in mourning." Thus his father wept for him. (Genesis 37:34,35)

If you've ever watched televised sporting events, you will know that slow-motion is rarely flattering. The facial expressions of handsome heroes who are slowed close to a standstill are often ugly. When we slow down the Scriptures and closely analyze the actions of Joseph's brothers, it's really ugly.

Their envy and jealousy poisoned them to a point of wanting to commit murder, then it changed to kidnapping, which necessitated lying, and they then dishonored their beloved father by laying the unbearable weight of *unnecessary* grief upon him. They took away his greatest reason for living. I wonder if they ever felt any guilt that their sin caused such needless, ongoing pain to their father. Perhaps they surmised that he would grieve for a time and then move on with life.

I received the following email from grieving parents (names and locations removed for privacy):

Dear Ray,

I have been reading your *Evidence Bible* for many years, listening to your CDs and happily support your ministry. It is full of useful information for witnessing and daily life. Today I need your wisdom.

We lost our youngest son, Andrew, on February 3rd of this year in a horrible dirt bike accident. He was hit by a train while traversing a short distance of track. A stupid mistake that cost him his life. There were three other young men with him, all are okay, except for the trauma of seeing a good friend killed. They and we are in counseling. We have been told many things. Like, there are no rules to grieving, it will take a long, long time to feel better, and this is the new normal.

There is no way to make sense of this tragedy. I have spent hours searching the scriptures. Over and over I read about pain and suffering. Jesus said in this world you will have troubles. Solomon said all life is vanity, a chasing after the wind. Then there is Job.

[Our son] was 23 years old and a senior...in Mechanical Engineering. He was well liked and had many friends. About 50 drove...to attend [his] celebration of life, an awesome tribute to him and the influence he had on his friends. We are so very proud of him and miss him terribly. We try to comfort ourselves with the knowledge that Andrew was saved and is in heaven with Jesus now. No longer suffering the pains of this life.

While my pain is nearly unbearable, my wife's pain is overwhelming and consuming. Her moods change in fractions of seconds and are intense. Often, like today, her grief and depression drag me down and I become virtually nonfunctional.

I know you do not have any answers. Our counselor is a wonderful Christian woman who lost her son about 2 years ago. So she is able to truly understand what we are going through. She helps the best she can.

My faith is strong but being tested. I can't find in the scriptures a reason to hope for the future.

I know this is a lot to lay on you given you do not even know us. But I am certain you have counseled many grieving people. So, I am simply hoping you can offer some hope, words I can cling to while I wait for the pain to lessen.

I replied:

Thank you for emailing me.

My heart breaks for you, but I am going to get to the point very quickly and share with you how I deal with grief. I have shared these thoughts with others, and the principle has worked for them.

The human mind is incredibly complex. I am not sure of the difference between the mind and the soul, but I do know that my thoughts often go into directions that I (my soul) don't want them to go. I'm not just talking about the sins of lust, bitterness, gossip, and unbelief that often invade my mind without invitation, I'm talking about the issue of grief.

A few years ago I lost my beloved mom and dad. I wept uncontrollably at their loss, and then I determined never to go down Grief Street again. When I get emotional thoughts about my mom and dad and feel a heaviness come with them that is almost unbearable, I shake it off and bring my thoughts into captivity. I have done my crying. I have grieved. It is over. I will not go down that road again because it overwhelms me.

I don't feel the slightest bit of guilt with this, and I have told my wife that when I go to be with the Lord she is to do the same thing. I would not like my death to bring unhappiness to those I love.

So Grief Street is totally out of bounds, because it is a dead end.

My advice would be to discipline yourself to say, "I will not go there. Ever." If I can do it with lust, bitterness, gossip, and unbelief, I can (with God's help) retain my joy —which according to Scripture is my strength.

This attitude, which some could see as flippant or at least lacking sensitivity, has a biblical basis:

And the LORD struck the child that Uriah's wife bore to David, and it became ill. David therefore pleaded with God for the child, and David fasted and went in and lay all night on the ground. So the elders of his house arose and went to him, to raise him up from the ground. But he would not, nor did he eat food with them. Then on the seventh day it came to pass that the child died. And the servants of David were afraid to tell him that the child was dead. For they said, "Indeed, while the child was alive, we spoke to him, and he would not heed our voice. How can we tell him that the child is dead? He may do some harm!"

When David saw that his servants were whispering, David perceived that the child was dead. Therefore David said to his servants, "Is the child dead?"

And they said, "He is dead."

So David arose from the ground, washed and anointed himself, and changed his clothes; and he went into the house of the LORD and worshiped. Then he went to his own house; and when he requested, they set food before him, and he ate. Then his servants said to him, "What is this that you have done? You fasted and wept for the child while he was alive, but when the child died, you arose and ate food."

And he said, "While the child was alive, I fasted and wept; for I said, 'Who can tell whether the LORD will be gracious to me, that the child may live?' But now he is dead; why should I fast? Can I bring him back again? I shall go to him, but he shall not return to me." (2 Samuel 12:15–23)

If you are weighed down by grief, may I encourage you to get up from the low ground of grief, wash and anoint yourself daily in God's Word, and change your clothes? Take off the garment of heaviness and replace it with the garment of praise. Give God the sacrifice of worship, as did David.

IT IS NOT GOOD

No one seems to really know why we say the words "good grief!" Some say it is a euphemism for "good G-d!" (blasphemy). Whatever the case, grief is *not* good. It is pain of the soul. The quicker it leaves, the better. So here are some practical things you can do to show grief the door.

The battleground is your mind. So busy it with other things. Plant so many plants in the garden that there is no room for weeds. Weeds don't do anything but soak up the soil's energy. Grieving doesn't do any lasting good. It just steals joy and soaks up your energy. It sucks the oxygen out of the room. To survive, you must open the door and run away from it into the fresh air of the promises of God.

You are a soldier of Christ. Bring your thoughts into captivity and put your eyes on the *real* battle. People are going to Hell. What are you doing about it? Are you looking to the past (which Philippians 3:13 says to forget), and not pressing on toward the mark of the high calling of God in Christ Jesus? Use the past as a footstool to look to the future. Stand on top of it. Overcome it and busy yourself in the task of evangelism. Could you be so overwhelmed with grief that you stand and do nothing while a child drowns in a swimming pool beside you? You could never defend yourself in court for such neglect of human duty. How could you and I defend ourselves before God if we do nothing while sinners are sinking into Hell?

Bring your thoughts into captivity and put your eyes on the real *battle. People are going to Hell.*

A. W. Tozer said, "Christians alone are in a position to rescue the perishing. We dare not settle down to try to live as if things were 'normal.' Nothing is normal while sin and lust and death roam the world, pouncing upon one and another till the whole population has been destroyed."

Busy yourself in good works. Immerse yourself in the Word and prayer, then keep yourself occupied in helping those around you with the comfort with which God has comforted you. Don't let the enemy have another moment of your time. It is too precious.

I wonder if Jacob, while in his grieving state, ever thought about Joseph's dreams. If he had continually "kept the matter in mind" (Genesis 37:11), and he believed them (that somehow God was going to work a miracle and bring them to pass), he may have been lifted above the weight of his grief.

But you don't have nebulous dreams by which you may overcome grief. You have the sure and true promises of God. Believe them with all of your heart, and make sure that your faith is evidenced by joy. That will take you through the day without being suffocated by grief.

But it's clear that Jacob didn't believe that God had given Joseph a glimpse of the future. Upon hearing what he thought was news of his beloved son's death, Jacob *refused* to be comforted. Charles Spurgeon said,

> When you meet with a person in great distress, you feel at once a desire to comfort him; that is to say, if you have an ordinarily tender heart. You cannot bear to see another in trouble without trying to minister to that diseased heart. But supposing that the person refuses to be comforted; then you are foiled. What can you do? It is as though you met with a hungry man, and offered him bread, but he rejected it. You tried to give him daintier food, but he scorned it. You asked him what he could eat, but he altogether refused to accept any form of nourishment. Then what could you do? Your cupboard might be full, and the door might be freely opened; but if the man would not eat, you could not remove his hunger.
>
> So, if a man in trouble refuses to be comforted, how are you to cheer and solace him? One man can lead a horse to the water, but a thousand cannot make him drink if he will not; and when a man in trouble refuses to be comforted, then lover and friend are put far from him, and his acquaintance into darkness. Indeed, they themselves soon want to be comforted, for disquietude is contagious; and, sometimes, those who come to comfort another, go away provoked by his perversity. Many a man, whose heart was full of pity, has at last become indignant,

and so has increased the sorrow which he intended to assuage; he has grown angry with the man who willfully put aside what was intended to encourage him.[3]

How good it is to see a person who is down accept a helping hand and lift themselves up. It is a victory for you and for them, but for the Christian it is even greater. It is God-glorifying when we believe His promises and walk on a deadly water that normally drowns the lost.

It is God-glorifying when we sleep in the storm, because the unsaved watch how we handle adversity. If a storm causes us to collapse just like it does to the unsaved, then Christianity is a waste of time. If it can't sustain us in life, how can it help us in death?

But Jesus did not die in vain. He defeated the enemy of death, and we stand upon death in victory with the sword of the Spirit in our hand. Goliath is dead and so is his taunting. Therefore, don't have a mind to listen to it. Be comforted by God's exceedingly great and precious promises.

Look at the wording of Scripture:

> But I do not want you to be ignorant, brethren, concerning those who have fallen asleep, *lest you sorrow as others who have no hope.* For if we believe that Jesus died and rose again, even so God will bring with Him those who sleep in Jesus.
>
> For this we say to you by the word of the Lord, that we who are alive and remain until the coming of the Lord will by no means precede those who are asleep. For the Lord Himself will descend from heaven with a shout, with the voice of an archangel, and with the trumpet of God. And the dead in Christ will rise first. Then we who are alive and remain shall be caught up together with them in the clouds to meet the Lord in the air. And thus we shall always be with the Lord. Therefore comfort one another

with these words. (1 Thessalonians 4:13–18, emphasis added)

We are not as those who have no hope. We should therefore not act as though we are.

REFUSING TO BE COMFORTED

We see the same wording with the Bethlehem mothers who lost their beloved children. They refused to be comforted:

> Then Herod, when he saw that he was deceived by the wise men, was exceedingly angry; and he sent forth and put to death all the male children who were in Bethlehem and in all its districts, from two years old and under, according to the time which he had determined from the wise men. Then was fulfilled what was spoken by Jeremiah the prophet, saying:

> "A voice was heard in Ramah,
> Lamentation, weeping, and great mourning,
> Rachel weeping for her children,
> Refusing to be comforted,
> Because they are no more." (Matthew 2:16–18)

How could there be any consolation? One moment the mothers were looking into the bright sparkling eyes of their beloved childen, and the next their precious offspring were gushing blood, thrust through with the cold, sharp steel of a Roman sword. This wasn't some terrible accident. It was murder, and there wasn't even hope of justice.

Why did God allow it? Why didn't He kill Herod before he spilled the blood of the innocent? Why didn't He warn the mothers in a dream? There is nothing too hard for Him. The only answer we have is that we don't know. All of us will eventually be struck by the cold blade of a loved one's death, horrific though the thought may be. When it comes, we must never refuse to be comforted. Jacob and those poor mothers didn't have the hope we have in Christ. We have the glorious promises of the Word of God, and particularly Romans 8:28. There's our comfort if we want it—the comfort of the Scriptures:

> For whatever things were written before were written for our learning, that we through the patience and comfort of the Scriptures might have hope. (Romans 15:4)

The Scriptures were written for our learning, so learn the lesson. Rejoice in hope. Grief is the most suffocating of ducks. Stand up and overcome the dark shadow of adversity. Hope in God's promises is the light in such a dark place. It is a glorious ray of comfort.

There is another aspect to Jacob's inconsolable grief. He was of the mistaken belief that his beloved son had been eaten by some vicious animal. Joseph was at the wrong place at the wrong time, and the *reason* for him being in that place at that time was that his father had sent him there. The Scriptures say that Jacob said to Joseph,

> "Please go and see if it is well with your brothers and well with the flocks, and bring back word to me." So he sent him out of the Valley of Hebron, and he went to Shechem. (Genesis 37:14)

The distance from Hebron to Shechem was around fifty miles. That's a long way to send a seventeen-year-old kid, alone, knowing that there had been trouble between the people of Shechem and his sons (see Genesis 34:25–30). It was a long way to send him knowing that there were the dangers of wild animals and rumors of slave traders. Perhaps Jacob was plagued not only with the knowledge that his son was dead, but also with the thought that he *sent* Joseph to his death. And maybe that added to his terrible grief.

THE GOOD GRIEF

However, there is one grief that is good. It's not a grief that destroys, but it is one that does weigh heavy on those who experience it. It doesn't grieve because a loved one has died. It grieves because *billions* are dying and going to Hell. They are heading for a terrible place that makes the sufferings of this life seem like a picnic. Jesus warned that it would be better to pull out your eye rather than let it cause you to end up there (see Matthew 5:29).

One meaning of the word "grief" is "a cause or occasion of keen distress or sorrow." Let me ask you a few probing questions. Do you *believe* what Jesus said about Hell? Are you a "believer"? Does it bother you that human beings who die in their sins will justly end up there? Is that a cause or occasion of keen distress or sorrow? It should be.

Grief is the most suffocating of ducks. Stand up and overcome the dark shadow of adversity.

It grieves me beyond words. It's the reason I write books, endlessly give out tracts, produce movies, and plead with God in prayer. It's the reason I preach in the open air and go out of my way to befriend strangers that I would rather not approach. If Hell didn't exist, I wouldn't bother doing any of these things. But I do because it does. That sort of grief motivates, and that's good.

Perhaps you are thinking that you (like Moses, Gideon, and Jeremiah) cannot speak. You don't know what to say. It's not your "gift." Let me then tell you about my friend Brandon Maya. When he was age sixteen, he was a normal active, fun-loving teenager, and worship leader in the youth group of his church. He wrote song lyrics, played the guitar, and went on mission trips. But one day in 2008 he collapsed at school.

Doctors initially thought that he suffered a head injury when he fell. But they later found that he collapsed because of an undetected brain aneurysm.

Brandon *cannot* speak. Neither can he feed himself. Nor can he move any part of his paralyzed body except for his right hand. Yet he is deeply concerned for the lost, has preached in the open air (through an automated voice on his laptop computer), and regularly gives out gospel tracts. If we say that we *cannot* speak to the lost, we don't know the meaning of the word. Brandon makes me feel ashamed of my whining about my fears.

Questions

1. What was your initial reaction to what Joseph's brothers did to their father? What one adjective would you use to describe what they did?

2. How many of the Ten Commandments did they break?

3. Have you ever felt overwhelmed by grief? Did you eventually overcome it? How?

4. Do you ever have serious thoughts about the fate of the unsaved?

5. What are you doing to reach them with the message of everlasting life?

Chapter Six

JOSEPH'S RED BLOOD

As we read the account of Joseph's life, he almost seems faultless. But we know better. He was from the offspring of Adam so we know that his heart was prone to sin. More than likely, therefore, he was tempted by Potiphar's wife because he had Adam's red blood in his veins. This doesn't take away from his godly character. Jesus was also tempted:

> For we do not have a High Priest who cannot sympathize with our weaknesses, but was in all points tempted as we are, yet without sin. (Hebrews 4:15)

But it wasn't just the goodness of Joseph's own heart that kept him from falling into the bed of sin. It was his fear of God.

When a generation forgets God, they lack the virtue of the fear of the Lord, which Scripture tells us is the beginning of wisdom (see Proverbs 9:10). To forsake the fear of God is to disconnect your car's brakes and push down on the accelerator. There is no restraint.

Plus, when someone is godless, their personal happiness becomes their primary concern. *They* are the center of the universe, and everything else revolves around them—their feelings, their rights, their wants, and their happiness. But the godly center on God's will, not their own. The foot is on the brake, and so personal happiness takes a backseat to righteousness. Life's decisions aren't based on what makes them happy, but on whether or not a certain thought or action is right: "Does this please God?" That was the motivation of Joseph.

Take, as an extreme example, the following incident that happened on Father's Day of 2018:

> Hong Kong (CNN) — A former nursing student murdered her parents before killing herself on Father's Day, according to Hong Kong police, who suggested her skin condition may have motivated the attack.
>
> An initial police report found that the 23-year-old had attacked her parents, inflicting fatal wounds to her father's chest, and her mother's chest, waist and legs.
>
> Their bodies were found by police after a relative called authorities, telling them that no one had answered the door at the apartment in Tuen Mun, a residential neighborhood of Hong Kong.
>
> A 30-centimeter knife, which was suspected to have been used in the attack, was recovered at the scene, police said.
>
> The couple's daughter Pang Ching-yu was also found dead at the scene. Police said they found a suicide note in Pang's bedroom saying she was bothered by long-term eczema.[4]

The reason she stabbed her parents to death was because she was being suffocated by ducks. Instead of doing what the godly do—trusting God that what was happening to her was working for her good—she was overwhelmed by hopeless-ness. On top of that, she blamed her parents for her condi-tion, and so she murdered them. She said online: "People with eczema giving birth to kids are worse than poor people giving birth to kids... If you're poor, you can rely on your own hard work. With eczema, sorry, you have to suffer (your whole life) with no change... there's nothing you can do ex-cept to wait and die," and that her "social life (was) all gone."

But to blame her innocent parents was terribly misguided. They didn't create her genes; God did. Perhaps that thought didn't enter her presumed godless mind.

We live in a fallen creation packed with terrible afflic-tions—from blindness to paralyzing and painful diseases... all ending in death. If our happiness is more important to us than righteousness, it won't be long until we become bitter and hateful—and, like Joseph's brothers, our hatred will enter-tain murder.

FRANCISCO AND JESSICA

When a nation loses its fear of God, it also loses all sense of modesty, or even a reason to be modest. We live in a society in which immodesty, fornication, pornography, blasphemy, homosexuality, and adultery are encouraged as normal hu-man behavior.

I spoke to a young couple not long ago about the things of God. I was riding my bike, with my dog on a special plat-form that I've created for him. He wears sunglasses, which elicits wonderful responses from those who see him. I have had many people call out, stop me, wave, take photos, and honk their car horn because he looks so cute. Consequently, I've been able to witness to many people because of my dog.

I pulled over and gave the couple a coin with the Ten Com-mandments on it. Their reaction was reasonably congenial, so I asked if they thought there was an afterlife. Francisco didn't, although he said he hadn't given it much thought. Neither had his girlfriend. So I said that if Heaven did exist, "Are you going there...are you a good person?"

Both Francisco and Jessica admitted that they had lied, he said he had stolen, they had both blasphemed, looked with lust, and unashamedly admitted that they were having sex.

I directed my attention to Francisco as Jessica listened, telling him that I wasn't judging him, but that he had admitted that he was a lying, thieving, blasphemous, fornicating adulterer at heart. When I asked them both if it concerned them that they would end up in Hell if God judged them by the Ten Commandments, he said it didn't bother him. But when I asked if he enjoyed pain (and gave examples, such as slamming his thumb in a door, or the dentist drill), it seemed to make my point. I explained the gospel, and asked them to think seriously about what we talked about. I pleaded with both of them to think about the value of life. If he was going to die that night, he would listen to the birds, look at the blue sky, think of the wonders of music, the taste of food, and of friendships, love, and laughter, and cry, "Oh, I don't want to die!"

I told him he was like a rich man who jumped from a sinking ship into the ocean, wearing an 80-pound gold belt. If he didn't repent and ask God to give him a new heart, his sins would drag him down to Hell.

Jessica had a Bible at home, and Francisco said he might have one. I then gave them each a Subway gift card, one of my books, and as I left I particularly prayed for Francisco. This was because Jessica was well-endowed and wore a very low-cut dress. She was a naked flame and he was a stick of dynamite every time he looked at her. Her immodesty lit his fuse. Previous generations didn't have such temptations, but this one has Potiphar's wife around every corner.

Joseph ran. Potiphar's fuse-lighting wife was daily in his face. He had no choice. He had to flee.

THE SCARY WOMAN

I was on the first leg of a twelve-hour trip to speak at the Billy Graham Training Center in North Carolina. The John Wayne airport in Orange County in Southern California was busy, but bearable, compared to the Los Angeles airport. It was almost pleasant in comparison. I had arrived two hours before our flight, so I left my bags with a friend while I went for a walk to stretch my legs.

When I got back to my seat, my heart sank. Not because my legs were still the same length, but because right next to my bags sat a woman who was wearing a pink and black pro-abortion march T-shirt. Of all the categories of people to whom I prefer not to witness, it is the category of Christian-hating, angry, anti-God, "pro-choice" women. In public.

I ignored my fears, and I asked her if she had attended the women's march. She told me that she did, along with half a million other women. She then added some expected disparaging remarks about the president. I bit my tongue, and made small talk with her for some time. But my fears began to grow because she was a rather loud lady, and everything she said could be heard fifty miles away.

That morning a well-known celebrity had tragically committed suicide. It was the second celebrity suicide in less than a week. More than 45,000 Americans each year are so overcome by life's suffocating ducks that they take their own lives, but only the famous make the headlines. I wanted to bring the subject up so that I could transition into talking about the afterlife, but I couldn't think of the celebrity's last name. To my delight, within seconds of me having that thought, she named him and brought up the subject of suicide. And so we talked about the tragedy of someone being in such despair that they take their life. That gave me the opening to ask if she believed in the afterlife.

Stephanie did, but she didn't believe in the existence of Hell. Even when I talked about Hitler and what he did to the Jews, she said we need only say we are sorry to God, because He was "all-forgiving."

I talked to her for a few moments about idolatry and how we gravitate to making up a god in our own image, one with no sense of justice or truth. I was all the while a little nervous because no one likes having their erroneous image of God destroyed. But that was my aim. I wanted to do what God commissioned Gideon to do —to destroy his father's idols. I needed to be as bold as Moses when he came down from the holy mountain and saw Israel deceived by idolatry. He threw the Ten Commandments at their sinful feet.

As long as sinners have a wrong view of God's nature, they won't see their need to repent and trust in Jesus.

As long as sinners have a wrong view of God's nature, they won't fear Him, nor will they see their need to repent and trust in Jesus. Why should they, if God is happy with humanity?

When I asked Stephanie if she was going to make it to Heaven—if she was a good person—she said she was.

As we went through the Commandments, she admitted that she had broken them but that God was forgiving. It was because she now had the knowledge of sin that I told her that she was right about God being forgiving, and that He had made provision for our forgiveness through the cross. I added that each of us need to repent and trust in Jesus alone.

When I gave her a copy of a book I had written on the subject of depression and suicide, she was delighted.

I was relieved, and thanked her for listening to me. When she then added that she liked talking about God, you could have knocked me over with a feather. None of my fears had been realized. As I left to board my flight I slipped a Subway gift card into her hand. Her expression was worth a thousand words.

As I waited in line, I looked at that dear woman as she chatted with someone on her phone, and prayed that God would bring her out of darkness into light.

The Subway card was my small way of expressing love. Jesus said to let our light shine before men (Matthew 5:16), and the way to let the light shine brightly is with our good works. An expression of love puts to silence the ignorance of foolish people (see 1 Peter 2:15). This isn't just to be generous. It isn't just because that's how God treats the whole of humanity. It's also because we want to reach them with the gospel, and if they can see the genuineness of our faith, they may listen to our words.

Questions

1. Do you fear God? If not, why not?

2. Have you ever been disappointed by the moral failings of a godly person you admired? Did it shake your faith in human beings or in God? Why?

3. What is your greatest fear when it comes to reaching out to the unsaved?

4. What should be more important to us—happiness or righteousness? Explain your reasoning.

5. When have you ever been tempted to put happiness above righteousness?

Chapter Seven

FAMINE IN THE LAND

In the book of Acts, Stephen was taking his hearers through a Bible study. As he breezed through the Old Testament stories, he gave us a Holy Spirit–inspired synopsis:

> And the patriarchs, becoming envious, sold Joseph into Egypt. But God was with him and delivered him out of all his troubles, and gave him favor and wisdom in the presence of Pharaoh, king of Egypt; and he made him governor over Egypt and all his house. Now a famine and great trouble came over all the land of Egypt and Canaan, and our fathers found no sustenance. But when Jacob heard that there was grain in Egypt, he sent out our fathers first. And the second time Joseph was made known to his brothers, and Joseph's family became known to the Pharaoh. Then Joseph sent and called his father Jacob and all his relatives to him, seventy-five people. (Acts 7:9–14)

Stephen was speaking to those who were so full of hatred, they were about to murder him. They listened until he told them that they had broken God's Law—then they blew a fuse (see Acts 7:53–59). As he spoke of the great famine, he said, "But when Jacob heard that there was grain in Egypt, he sent out our fathers first" (Acts 7:12).

There was grain in Egypt. There was hope that they would live! That is the simplicity of our message. There is a famine in the land. The world is starving to death, but Jesus Christ is the Bread of Life (John 6:35). We therefore long to bring people to the Savior. Scripture promises that those who come to Him will never hunger.

My dog, Sam, and I had been out on my bike one morning and had seen only one person, and he didn't speak English. I decided to go out again at about 10 a.m. and approached a man who was on his phone. He said that he would give me an interview when he finished. I took it that he would wind down talking with his girlfriend, so I stood a polite distance from him and waited...and waited. After about twenty or thirty minutes I waved goodbye to him, handed him a gift card, and left.

Around 2 o'clock that afternoon Sam began pestering me to go out again. As I walked out to the bike I thought of four good reasons why I was going out again: 1) I wasn't doing anything important that afternoon; 2) It was good exercise; 3) It made my dog happy; and 4) I would be able to share the message of everlasting life with sinners headed for Hell. Besides, I might get an interview with someone that would be watched by thousands if not millions. (Our YouTube channel at that time had just over 55,000,000 views.)

I prayed that God would give me people whose hearts had been prepared for the gospel. But as I began riding, my enthusiasm waned a little. I had a head wind and felt physically exhausted.

About ten minutes later, I saw two young men on a grassy area, who were drinking beer. There must've been a dozen empty cans at their feet. They were clearly suspicious of my bold, "Hi, guys!" approach, but both took a Ten Commandment coin. One of them said, "This is cool, but I'm an atheist." When I asked him if he really believed that nothing created everything, he was a little taken aback and asked what I meant. I said that there was either something in the beginning or nothing, but that nothing couldn't create anything because it was nothing. "You are probably an agnostic—you simply don't know." He said, "I'm an agnostic then." They were polite, but when I asked if I could talk to them for a few minutes, one of them said, "I think you had better leave." I said, "Sure. Before I go, I'd like to give you each a gift card for dinner." They refused, which was a little strange, but they thanked me for my kindness. As I rode away I realized that they probably thought I was an undercover police officer.

SHE DIDN'T MISS

In 2017, a young man who craved fame had his girlfriend shoot a bullet at him while he protected himself with an encyclopedia:

> According to court documents, the couple had prepared the stunt hoping for it to go viral. Police said the couple set up two cameras outside their Halstad home. Their 3-year-old daughter and almost 30 other people were watching.
>
> Perez, who was pregnant at the time with their second child, was heard in the video telling Ruiz she could not shoot him. Ruiz asked his girlfriend to shoot him with a .50 caliber handgun while he held an encyclopedia to his chest. He assured her that he had done it before with a different book.
>
> "I can't do it babe," she said. "I'm so scared. [inaudible] my heart is beating out of [inaudible]."

"Babe, if I kill you what's gonna happen to my life. Like no, this isn't OK," she said. "I don't want to be responsible."

"As long as you hit the book, you'll be fine. Come on," Ruiz told her.

The bullet went through the book, killing Ruiz on June 26, 2017 . . . In another video released by prosecutors, Ruiz was heard saying he could die from the stunt but had "confidence that my girlfriend will hit the book and not me."[5]

She *did* hit the book. But the bullet when straight through it and killed him. That left his girlfriend without a provider, put her into prison, left their kids without a father or mother, and he more than likely lost his soul. All for the hollow praise of men.

Those multiple tragedies happened because he miscalculated what the bullet could do.

When professing atheists deny the existence of God, they are making a massive miscalculation. They think unbelief will protect them. It won't.

Psalm 94 begins with a cry for God to fire the bullet of His wrath at the wicked:

O LORD God, to whom vengeance belongs—
O God, to whom vengeance belongs, shine forth!
Rise up, O Judge of the earth;
Render punishment to the proud.
LORD, how long will the wicked,
How long will the wicked triumph?
They utter speech, and speak insolent things;
All the workers of iniquity boast in themselves.
(Psalm 94:1–4)

Then the Scriptures reveal a major delusion of the wicked. They miscalculate the nature of God, and from there they minimize the depth of His power:

Yet they say, "The LORD does not see,
Nor does the God of Jacob understand."
Understand, you senseless among the people;
And you fools, when will you be wise?
He who planted the ear, shall He not hear?
He who formed the eye, shall He not see?
He who instructs the nations, shall He not correct,
He who teaches man knowledge?
The LORD knows the thoughts of man,
That they are futile. (Psalm 94:7–11)

When any reasonable atheist is pressed as to what he believes, he will always come down to the thought that he can't "know" there is no God, because he's not omniscient. His knowledge is limited. An article about the world's most famous atheist was headlined "Richard Dawkins: I can't be sure God does not exist." Speaking of a debate about the existence of God, the article said:

> There was surprise when Prof Dawkins acknowledged that he was less than 100 per cent certain of his conviction that there is no creator.
>
> The philosopher Sir Anthony Kenny, who chaired the discussion, interjected: "Why don't you call yourself an agnostic?" Prof Dawkins answered that he did.
>
> An incredulous Sir Anthony replied: "You are described as the world's most famous atheist."
>
> Prof Dawkins said that he was "6.9 out of seven" sure of his beliefs.
>
> "I think the probability of a supernatural creator existing is very very low," he added.[6]

Just after I left the nervous and inebriated ex-atheist and his friend, I rode past two young men who were so fascinated by Sam that I heard one of them called out, "The dog is wearing sunglasses!"

I stopped my bike, turned around, went back and gave them a coin with the Ten Commandments on it. One of them said that it was very cool, and that he was a Christian, but he hadn't been born again. The other said he didn't know much about God. When I asked them to come on camera, they said that they definitely wouldn't; they were too shy.

When I asked permission to speak to them for a few moments off camera, they were very congenial. Their names were Jeff and Juan. Jeff was wearing a cross, so I asked him what it meant to him. He said that it was just a gift and didn't mean anything. Juan said that he didn't believe in the after-life but that he wasn't an atheist. When he said, "I believe in science. Nature made everything," I said that it was scientifically impossible for nature to make itself. "For nature to make itself, it would have had to be preexistent to make itself *before* it made itself—which is ludicrous." Juan nodded and said, "I understand what you're saying."

They had just been talking about these things, and he hoped somebody would stop and enlighten them.

As we went through the Commandments, they both realized they would be in big trouble on Judgment Day. When I shared the good news of the cross, Juan opened wide his eyes and said that they had just been talking about these sorts of things, and that he had hoped that somebody would stop and enlighten them.

They were showing interest, so I took advantage of their openness to share biblical truths. I asked if they could think of anything in which they had faith. After they thought for a moment I offered, "How about pilots? You get into planes and trust your life to people you don't even know. You don't walk into the cockpit and demand to see their credentials or do a breathalyzer test, in case they'd been drinking alcohol. You trust your life to them without a second thought."

PLAIN FAITH

I prefer to fly in large planes because every day there are 87,000 flights in the US without incident. However, many put their faith in smaller planes because they are more convenient. But there's a little problem that may make us think twice before we step into them:

> Nearly 45,000 people have been killed in crashes of small airplanes and helicopters since 1964, and while federal investigators overwhelmingly blame pilots, *USA TODAY* found repeated instances in which crashes, deaths and injuries were caused by defective parts and dangerous designs.
>
> The findings cast doubt on government rulings and reveal the inner workings of an industry hit so hard by legal claims that it sought and won liability protection from Congress.
>
> Our three-part *USA TODAY* investigation found wide-ranging defects have persisted for years as manufacturers covered up problems, lied to federal regulators and failed to remedy known malfunctions.[7]

Then I spoke to Jeff and Juan about how doctors give us pills and tell us to take two every four hours. We trust our lives to the medical profession with hardly a second thought.

But there's also a little problem with putting our trust in the medical profession:

> Medical errors are the third leading cause of death in the U.S., after heart disease and cancer, causing at least 250,000 deaths every year, according to an analysis out Tuesday indicating that patient safety efforts fall far short.
>
> "People don't just die from heart attacks and bacteria, they die from system-wide failings and poorly coordinated

care," says the study's lead author, Dr. Martin Makary, a professor of surgery and health policy at Johns Hopkins University School of Medicine. "It's medical care gone awry."[8]

I mentioned how we trust our lives to elevators, but that they too can sometimes let us down. An article titled "Are elevators really hazardous to your health?" explains:

It's a question many people are asking after two elevator accidents killed two women in two weeks. Last week, Annette Lujan was crushed by an elevator at Cal State Long Beach after she tried to climb out of a stuck car. On Wednesday, Suzanne Hart died after an elevator door in her Manhattan office building closed on her leg as she was stepping in and dragged her body up into the elevator shaft.

The incidents were tragic but also very rare. According to ConsumerWatch.com, "U.S. elevators make 18 billion passenger trips per year." Those trips result in about 27 deaths annually, according to estimates from the U.S. Bureau of Labor Statistics and the Consumer Product Safety Commission.[9]

I asked the two young men, "You know what death is, don't you?" They both looked mystified by the question. "It's the arresting officer that drags us as criminals before the Judge of the Universe, to give an account of violating God's Law. And when we're found guilty, we will be cast into God's prison, a terrible place call Hell, without parole."

THE MIDLIFE CRISIS

It's not easy to have a midlife crisis. This is because we don't know when we are at the middle point of life. My crisis came when I was twenty-one years old—which wasn't my midlife.

The term "midlife crisis" was coined by Elliott Jaques in 1965, and is commonly described by Wikipedia as "psychological crisis brought about by events that highlight a person's growing age, inevitable mortality, and possibly shortcomings of accomplishments in life."

Notice the words "inevitable mortality." In other words, we realize that we are going to die, and we can supposedly do nothing about it.

Human beings have an intuition for evasive action. If we see an 18-wheeler truck heading for us, we take evasive action. If we are in our right mind, we get out of the way.

It would seem that all we can do when it comes to death is eat healthy and get plenty of exercise. But that's not getting out of the way of the truck; it's merely stepping back from it to prolong the inevitable. We are still in its path.

Death is the arresting officer that drags us as criminals before the Judge of the Universe.

But the Bible is unique in that it tells us that we can take evasive action because of what God has already done. It tells us that death is capital punishment. The Judge of the universe proclaimed the death sentence upon the human race. We are waiting to be executed. The Scriptures say that "the soul who sins shall die" (Ezekiel 18:20). We have each violated God's Law and we await execution.

However, Jesus came and destroyed the power of death. The Scriptures say that Jesus Christ has abolished death; it was not possible for death to hold Him (see 2 Timothy 1:10; Acts 2:24).

The world calls death "The Grim Reaper." Its sharp sickle cuts down every man and woman irrespective of their race, color, or creed. Every hair that goes gray or falls from a balding head, every eye that loses sharpness, ear that loses hearing, or skin that wrinkles, is nature's warning that God is serious about sin. Deadly serious. As each member of the body crumbles, it is a frightful warning sign that death is approaching, and *that* should be a wake-up call for the gospel. But for most it's not. They need the wrath of the Law to show them that something even more horrific than death awaits them if they die in their sins.

With a famine in the land, they were hopeless and helpless—about to starve to death. But there was grain in Egypt.

After sharing all these biblical truths, I left a grateful Jeff and Juan each with coins, a signed book, information about our movies, and a gift card.

I thanked God for such a great time, and for some reason had the energy of a teenager as I rode my bike home.

Questions

1. What was it that angered Stephen's hearers (see Acts 7:53–59)? Why did it have that effect?

2. According to Psalm 94, what is a major delusion of the wicked?

3. Why can a professing atheist never be sure that God doesn't exist?

4. Name five things that most people trust, almost without question.

5. Did a "midlife crisis" (realizing your mortality) have any influence in bringing you to the cross? Give details.

Chapter Eight

THE EGYPTIAN HERALD

If it bleeds it leads, but hot gossip comes in neck-and-neck. Both are sure winners. If word of a handsome young slave sexually harassing the wife of a respected captain in the Pharaoh's guard become public, it was certainly hot news.

Sexual Predator Arrested

Egypt — A trusted slave of the Potiphar family was arrested by authorities today and held without bail on a charge of attempted rape. His master brought the charges against him saying that the crime was a personal betrayal. He had purchased the Hebrew, Joseph Jacobson, and trusted him with managing his entire estate and yet Jacobson had tried to rape his wife.

She told her husband that while the two were alone in the house, the youth had attempted to force himself on her and ran when she yelled for help. The accused maintained his innocence, saying that he was a trustworthy servant and would never do such a thing to dishonor his god. The Hebrew claims to have been kidnapped and sold to

Ishmaelites, before being purchased by Potiphar on the open market.

There was an independent testimony of his innocence:

And his master saw that the Lord was with him and that the Lord made all he did to prosper in his hand. So Joseph found favor in his sight, and served him. Then he made him overseer of his house, and all that he had he put under his authority. So it was, from the time that he had made him overseer of his house and all that he had, that the Lord blessed the Egyptian's house for Joseph's sake; and the blessing of the Lord was on all that he had in the house and in the field. Thus he left all that he had in Joseph's hand, and he did not know what he had except for the bread which he ate.

Now Joseph was handsome in form and appearance. And it came to pass after these things that his master's wife cast longing eyes on Joseph, and she said, "Lie with me." But he refused and said to his master's wife, "Look, my master does not know what is with me in the house, and he has committed all that he has to my hand. There is no one greater in this house than I, nor has he kept back anything from me but you, because you are his wife. How then can I do this great wickedness, and sin against God?" (Genesis 39:3–9)

However, this testimony wasn't allowed to be submitted in court because slaves have no rights in Egypt. Jacobson was incarcerated for an undisclosed time as a sexual predator.

When Potiphar's wife accosted him, Joseph found himself between a rock and a hard place. All he could do was to try to stay away from her, and if he had to be near her, he would make sure that they weren't alone (verse 10). But one day he found himself between the devil and the deep Red Sea:

But it happened about this time, when Joseph went into the house to do his work, and none of the men of the house was inside, that she caught him by his garment, saying, "Lie with me." But he left his garment in her hand, and fled and ran outside. And so it was, when she saw that he had left his garment in her hand and fled outside, that she called to the men of her house and spoke to them, saying, "See, he has brought in to us a Hebrew to mock us. He came in to me to lie with me, and I cried out with a loud voice. And it happened, when he heard that I lifted my voice and cried out, that he left his garment with me, and fled and went outside." (verses 11–15)

Potiphar's wife was a Jezebel. Her covetous eyes were full of adultery. She said, "See, he has brought in to us a Hebrew to mock us." In doing so she maligned her own husband as being culpable when it came to the supposed rape. She was manipulative, obviously wanting Potiphar to feel responsible for the incident so that he would punish Joseph:

So she kept his garment with her until his master came home. Then she spoke to him with words like these, saying, "The Hebrew servant whom you brought to us came in to me to mock me; so it happened, as I lifted my voice and cried out, that he left his garment with me and fled outside."

So it was, when his master heard the words which his wife spoke to him, saying, "Your servant did to me after this manner," that his anger was aroused. Then Joseph's master took him and put him into the prison, a place where the king's prisoners were confined. And he was there in the prison. But the Lord was with Joseph and showed him mercy, and He gave him favor in the sight of the keeper of the prison. And the keeper of the prison committed to Joseph's hand all the prisoners who were in the prison; whatever they did there, it was his doing. The keeper of the prison did not look into anything that was under Joseph's authority, because the Lord was with him; and whatever he did, the Lord made it prosper. (verses 16–23)

A garment got Joseph into trouble with his brothers, and a garment got him into trouble with his master. Both were through no fault of his own.

Joseph wasn't sinless. He had red blood in his veins. But he had the good sense to stay away from temptation. In what we commonly call "The Lord's Prayer," Jesus told us to pray that God doesn't lead us into temptation. He spoke from His own experience. The Father led Jesus into the wilderness to be tempted by the devil. If you can, avoid His having to do that. Bible says "*if need be*, you have been grieved by various trials" (1 Peter 1:6). God led Jesus into the wilderness, and into other less-than-exciting situations, to teach Him obedience:

Though He was a son, yet He learned obedience by the things which He suffered. And having been perfected, He became the author of eternal salvation to all who obey Him. (Hebrews 5:8)

He came to suffer, and suffering the temptation in the wilderness prepared Him for great battle in Gethsemane and the unspeakable horror of the cross.

We are sinners and should therefore want to avoid being tempted. Joseph tried faithfully to avoid Potiphar's wife, and he did so for a time. But one day he fell into her trap. They were found alone.

Our lesson is to never be alone with sin—especially sexual sin. It's a vicious Venus flytrap. Always bring God into your situation. Let Him take you by the hand and run. Flee, because every second you stay in sin's presence the more chance it has of overpowering you. Joseph ran. David didn't. Both got into big trouble, but Joseph had God's smile and kept free from sin. David caused God to frown and that led to the death of his child and brought chaos for the rest of his days. Let his life speak to you. Don't follow in his steps.

When the ducks come in the form of trials or temptations, stand tall. Don't be a pushover. Stand with your loins girded about with truth. Don't compromise with the father of lies. Keep your garment in hand and keep it clean.

We are targeted, not just by a God-hating world, but by demonic forces seeking to suffocate us. That's why Scripture tells us to put on the whole armor of God so we will be able to stand: "And having done all, to stand" (Ephesians 6:13). If you fall, get back up. When lust is thrown at you, use your sword to cut it down before it can stain your garment. Do the same with anger, bitterness, hatred, greed, pride, envy, jealousy, and doubt.

We are targeted, not just by a God-hating world, but by demonic forces seeking to suffocate us.

Potiphar's wife got close enough to Joseph to take hold of his garment. She may take you with her eyes and say, "Let us take our fill of love," but don't let her deceive you. Lust is not a bedfellow of love. It is selfish; it is a fire that burns. Her desire to be with Joseph turned to a vicious hatred when he refused to yield to sin. She hated him because he wouldn't compromise. His righteousness was an offense to her. And like Herod's adulterous mistress, she then wanted his head on a plate.

The Bible says that we wrestle not against flesh and blood but against principalities and powers and spiritual wickedness in high places (Ephesians 6:12). Believe the Bible when it says that we fight demonic forces that want to destroy you. Don't compromise in any way. Don't lie, don't steal, don't lust, covet, or dishonor your parents; don't have a heart of unbelief, and don't gossip about anyone. Bite your tongue off, pluck your eye out, or cut off your hand before you give it to sin.

THE URGENCY OF THE WARNING

Pastor Bruce Garner is a wonderful Bible teacher. He said regarding 1 Corinthians 6:18,

> Did you know on 9/11 the people in the second tower had quite a while to save themselves? But a false announcement was made in the second tower that all was well and they should stay at their desks. Some managers chose to be good company men and women, get their heads down and keep working. And many more could've been saved in those express elevators if they did what the majority did and sensed that something disastrous was going on and decided, "I'll get yelled at later. I'm getting out of here now!" and they fled.
>
> If an airliner is coming into your building, there is no strength, there is no weapon, there is no amount of physical fitness that can save you. The only way to live is to be as far away from that building as you possibly can. That's the urgency in Paul's warning here for you to flee from sexual immorality. Every other sin a person commits is outside the body, but the sexually immoral person sins against his own body—that's why sexual immorality is so destructive.
>
> Joseph was a slave. He couldn't run too far, and we are in the same restricted predicament. Sin seeks to seduce us from within and from without. The world flashes its bright lights. The devil tempts us, and the flesh loves the lights as well as the temptation. It's as weak as water. That's why we must cultivate a good conscience before God, always being aware that sin's attraction is there because we

love it. It is your own heart that you have to guard with all diligence. Shut that door and sin will have no dominion over you.

Charles Spurgeon said, "If you will tell me when God permits a Christian to lay aside his armor, I will tell you when Satan has left off temptation. Like the old knights in war time, we must sleep with helmet and breastplate buckled on, for the arch-deceiver will seize our first un-guarded hour to make us his prey."[10]

Questions

1. Have you ever been blamed for something you didn't do? How did it make you feel?

2. Has your garment of righteousness (taking a biblical stand) ever gotten you into trouble? Give details.

3. Why should we ask that God not lead us into temptation?

4. Explain the difference between Joseph and Potiphar's wife and David and Bathsheba. What did David lack?

5. How can we best cultivate a good conscience? Describe the working of the conscience. Can the conscience always be relied upon?

Chapter Nine

YOU HAVE TO WORK AT IT

By serving the pleasures of sin, the world walks into the path of stampeding elephants. The Bible warns, "Fools, because of their transgression, and because of their iniquities, were afflicted" (Psalm 107:17). Whatever a man sows, he reaps. Lying, stealing, rape, hatred, adultery, fornication, lust, etc., have deadly consequences in this life, and more so in the next. But the Christian stays clear of those traps. He has the Scriptures to show him sin's devastating results, a fear of God, his primed conscience, and the good sense to stop him from fooling with it.

Think for a moment what was at stake when Potiphar's wife offered Joseph sexual pleasure. If he had turned his back on God and secretly began to serve sin, he would have kept his trusted servant job and its illicit daytime benefits. He would not have ended up in prison. He would, therefore, have not interpreted the dreams of the baker and the butler, and not have consequently been exalted to the right hand of Pharaoh. Neither would he have delivered Egypt from famine, and brought all of Israel into the land of Goshen. Moses would not have been born in Egypt, and the Red Sea would not have been opened with the rod of Moses freeing the Israelites from slavery.

Never let sin steal the future that God has planned for you. What you decide now about serving sin will determine your future, as well as the future of others who may come into the kingdom through your faithful witness. You are a "certain" person for others.

Life is too precious to be distracted by the foolishness of unlawful pleasure. You get only one chance with life. Deny yourself. Take up the cross daily and closely follow Jesus.

THE JOY OF DOING NOTHING

So many marriages have been destroyed because of a lack of the beneficial virtue of the principle of self-denial and following Jesus. I have often heard the words "Marriage is hard" from the world. But when I've heard it said by Christians, I've flinched and thought, "No, it's not; it's easy." At the same time I've wondered if I'm being proud, simplistic, or unrealistic when it comes to marriage.

I can understand why it's hard for the world. Unregenerate human nature is selfish. It starts in infancy screaming to be fed. It believes that it's the center of the universe and needs to be treated as such. As the child grows it should be continually corrected, and if this instruction doesn't find root, the child will grow to be a great tree of self-centeredness. When two people come together in marriage with two monsters of selfishness still wanting their own way, it's only a matter of time until they devour each other.

Christians, however, are those whose monster has been destroyed at the cross. They have been crucified with Christ and the life they now live in the flesh is kind, selfless, and loving. And that's all that's necessary to overcome the difficulties that constantly beset the average marriage.

A friend sent me the following thoughtful joke: A wife asked her husband, "Are you sometimes surprised at how little people change?" The husband answered, "Actually, the process is the same. They just have tiny clothes."

The husband's reply completely changes our interpretation of the wife's question. The biblical reply to the question of our salvation can also change our perspective. For example, the rich young ruler asked what "good thing" he should do to find everlasting life (see Matthew 19:16). When it comes to that question, we mustn't allow any ambiguity. There is nothing "good" that we can do to be saved. Yet millions are sure they are on the right path when they embrace self-righteousness as a means of salvation. They believe that they have to "do" something to be saved, that salvation can be earned.

Life is too precious to be distracted by the foolishness of unlawful pleasure.

Our answer to them is that the good thing has already been done at the cross. We need not "do" anything except to accept the offer of salvation. Eternal life is a free gift, and the knowledge that it is free is freeing in itself, because it means that we can rest in Jesus. We don't have to work for anything. All the hard work has been done. Then we simply have to keep that which we have in Christ by holding onto Him.

UNLAWFUL SEXUAL PLEASURE

Early in 2018, a British newspaper carried a story titled "Pervert used pen camera to secretly take photos up woman's skirt in McDonald's." They reported:

Matthew Lewis sat next to the woman, in her 30s, and started showing her holiday pictures. Another woman spotted under-table images of her appearing on his phone. Lewis, of Brighton, denied outraging public decency but was convicted and given seven months' jail.[11]

Perversion isn't confined to that part of the world. Another man recently used a camera here in Southern California to do a similar thing. He filmed a woman actually removing her skirt. He then had the film distributed to sexual perverts who paid to watch it. This film wasn't a dirty little secret like the under-the-table MacDonald's video. It was legitimized by being rated "R" by the government. The "R" meant that the film was restricted to adults, because of its "nudity for sexual purposes." Of course, this was just Hollywood doing what it does every day.

As the fear of God has dissipated—like the fading rays of the sun at sunset—the world has sunk into moral darkness.

What then is the difference between the imprisoned English pervert, and Hollywood's perverted professional pimps who are free to make big money by selling their over-the-counter films to other perverts?

Is it that the man filmed a woman without her permission? So the problem wasn't his perversion, but rather that he lacked the ability to find women who would be willing to legally prostitute themselves.

This could have been easily solved. Instead of being sent to prison for "outraging public decency," Matthew Lewis should have been sent to Hollywood to earn a living. There, he could have pursued a legal career of finding loose ladies who don't mind being exploited by men, if the pay is right. In Hollywood, he could even rise to be a wealthy and legitimate film producer, just like Harvey Weinstein.

LEGITIMIZING ADULTERY

It wasn't too long ago that society had Joseph's attitude about adultery. To commit the act was to sin against God. It was to betray marital trust. But as the fear of God has dissipated—like the fading rays of the sun at sunset—the world has sunk into moral darkness. Adultery has become normalized:

> He receives regular death threats, websites are devoted to his demise, the Vatican has sent letters of complaint and the Queen of Spain has sued him.
>
> The man in question is not a criminal, a terrorist or a dictator. Instead, he is the businessman behind the world's biggest website for extramarital affairs.
>
> Noel Biderman is the Canadian founder of Ashley Madison, a controversial but globally popular adultery website that connects married men and women and discretely enables them to have affairs.
>
> Famed for its catchy motto—"Life is short. Have an affair"—the dating service is free for women but paying for men. Its array of features include virtual "winks," instant messaging and "travelling" services for members seeking an affair during business trips.
>
> Its mobile app uses GPS technology to track down the nearest available potential lover...
>
> But Mr Biderman ultimately believes that the human race is simply not biologically programmed to remain faithful—and that this can be good for a marriage.
>
> "People have affairs because we're not engineered for monogamy," he said. "Monogamy didn't come about from some great scientific research. If anything, the current social science tells us the opposite."[12]

He is right in concluding that our sinful nature isn't engineered for monogamy. It's engendered for sin. We drink iniquity like water. Our eyes are like those of Potiphar's wife

—clamoring for adultery. Without the restraint of the knowledge of God, we would grab the garment of anyone we desired.

The preceding article was titled "Adultery is good for your marriage—if you don't get caught, says infidelity website boss." The problem is that we *do* get caught. The eyes of the Lord are in every place keeping watch on the evil and the good (Proverbs 15:3). And adultery is not *good*. It's *evil* in God's pure eyes, and He warns in His Word that adulterers will not inherit the kingdom of God:

> Do you not know that the unrighteous will not inherit the kingdom of God? Do not be deceived. Neither fornicators, nor idolaters, nor adulterers, nor homosexuals, nor sodomites, nor thieves, nor covetous, nor drunkards, nor revilers, nor extortioners will inherit the kingdom of God. (1 Corinthians 6:9,10)

Joseph didn't have the Word of God. He didn't even have the Seventh Commandment written in stone by the finger of God. But he *did* have the work of the Law written on his heart (Romans 2:15), and that is what kept him from sin.

Faith consoles us in our most solemn hour by reminding us that Heaven is in complete control.

It was because Joseph refused to commit adultery that he was cast into prison and bore the label of a sexual predator, even though he was innocent of any crime. And just as he excelled in Potiphar's household, so he proved himself to be a model prisoner. He still had his trust in God.

Faith shines the light of hope in the darkest of prisons. It consoles us in our most solemn hour by reminding us that Heaven is in complete control—no matter how out of control things on earth may seem. Faith in God is the eye of the hurricane; it is our place of peace. Nothing escapes His permissive will. He is never taken by surprise. He has promised that He is working all things together for our good, because we love Him and we are called according to His purpose (Romans 8:28).

Never let life overwhelm you. It's easy to allow that to happen, because almost every day brings with it new and sometimes frightening trials. Our lesson from the story of this young and honorable Hebrew is simply to trust in the Lord with all of our heart and not lean on our own understanding. This is because, to our finite mind, what we are going through makes no sense.

Romans 8:28 ends with the condition "to those who are the called according to His purpose." Reaching out to the lost is prioritized in God's purpose. That was expressed once and for all in the cross. The fact that we are surrounded by dying sinners should keep evangelism as our priority. If the enemy can't remove it from our focus, he may try another tactic. He will have us dilute the medicine. Many nowadays neglect the weightier matters of the Law—they fail to talk about sin, righteousness, and judgment.

In case you are hesitant to talk about sin and its consequences, let me tell you about two incidents. According to the Associated Press, in July 2018 a German pharmacist was thrown in jail for twelve years for diluting cancer drugs.

A court in western Germany has sentenced a pharmacist to 12 years in prison for diluting cancer drugs on a massive scale in order to finance his luxury lifestyle.

In its ruling Friday, the Essen regional court said defendant Peter S. had manipulated at least 14,000 drugs, the quality of which was "not insignificantly" diminished. The offenses took place in nearby Bottrop between 2012 and 2016...

The defendant allegedly obtained more than 50 million euros ($58 million) through the fraud, and used the money to build a villa with a large water slide.[13]

Back in August 2001, *The New York Times* said it was greed that drove another pharmacist to do the same thing:

"Everybody I've talked to is just unbelieving aghast, and just can't believe this kind of thing could happen in the United States," said Dr. Fred DeFeo, chairman of council of the Missouri State Medical Association. "It is certainly possible that some have had cancers that could have been cured that weren't.".…

The F.B.I. has said that homicide or manslaughter charges were possible if investigators linked the diluted drugs to a death.

More than 1,000 people have called an F.B.I. hot line, and two civil suits have been filed. Many people say they are agonizing over the prospect that they or their loved ones may have been deceived.

"The thought of a person doing that is devastating—to shorten a person's life even one minute is too much," said William Van Sant, 56, of Independence, Mo., whose wife, Rachel, received Taxol from Mr. Courtney's pharmacy to treat her endometrial cancer. Mrs. Van Sant died last year after her three chemotherapy treatments were unsuccessful.[14]

It is unthinkable that any human being could be so callous as to betray the trust of those who were so dependent on their honesty. Yet think of the many contemporary preachers who water down the message of the gospel. In doing so they remove from it its curative properties. When we refuse to talk about sin, righteousness, and judgment for any reason, we are no better than a betrayer of cancer patients. Those who do so are devoid of empathy. Many prosperity preachers have lined their pockets because of an ear-tickling gospel—that's not only *motivated* by greed, it *promotes* greed. It is both the fear of God and the love for sinners that should make us tremble at such evil.

Questions

1. Specify what Joseph would have missed if he had chosen to commit adultery.

2. What does it practically mean to deny yourself, take up the cross daily, and closely follow Jesus?

3. How would you know if your "monster" has been destroyed at the cross? What evidence would be seen?

4. How would you describe the fear of God? What are the results of possessing it? (See Proverbs 16:6.)

5. Have you ever heard a diluted gospel presentation? What was missing?

Chapter Ten

THE TRAGIC SADNESS

God has placed within mankind a sense of excitement when it comes to searching for buried treasures. Dogs, cats, and horses couldn't care less about gold, diamonds, pearls, or great riches that lie in sunken ships off the coast of some tropical island. *We* do, because there's a sense of adventure when searching for hidden treasure.

And so it is with God's Word. The psalmist said, "I rejoice at Your word as one who finds great treasure" (Psalm 119:162).

As we have seen, there is great treasure in the life of Joseph. There are hidden gems of biblical truth in the typology and symbolism as we uncover hidden references to Jesus and His incredible love demonstrated at the cross.

> It came to pass after these things that the butler and the baker of the king of Egypt offended their lord, the king of Egypt. And Pharaoh was angry with his two officers, the chief butler and the chief baker. (Genesis 40:1,2)

In the narrative of the baker and the butler, we have a picture of the state of all humanity, the exclusivity of salvation by grace through faith, and the tragic error of self-righteousness.

Both the butler and the baker had seriously offended their lord, and because of that offense, he was angry with them.

When I ask unsaved people if God is angry them, rarely do they say that He is. On the contrary, if anything, they think God is happy with them. This is in direct opposition to Holy Scripture which says that He "is angry with the wicked every day" (Psalm 7:11). His wrath abides on them, and every time they sin that wrath justly increases (Romans 2:5,6). They are enemies of God in their minds because of wicked works, children of wrath, for whom Hell opens wide its mouth.

In the narrative of the baker and the butler, we have a picture of the state of all humanity.

Such thoughts are offensive to the unsaved, until God's Law in the hand of the Spirit does its illuminating work. Until such a time, religious sinners will religiously go about to establish their own righteousness, being ignorant of the righteousness which is of God.

The convincing agent for the baker and the butler—that they had offended their lord—was the stark reality that he had put them in prison:

> So he put them in custody in the house of the captain of the guard, in the prison, the place where Joseph was confined. And the captain of the guard charged Joseph with them, and he served them; so they were in custody for a while. (Genesis 40:3,4)

No matter how much they tried to trivialize their offenses, they couldn't argue with the fact that they had been taken from a palace and locked in a cold dungeon. Their reality was undeniable evidence of their wrongdoing.

Sinners may argue that they haven't offended God, that all is well between them and Heaven, but they can't argue with the realty that they are being held in a cold dungeon on death row.

How angry is God at sinners? Angry enough to proclaim the death sentence upon every son and daughter of Adam. They are going to die, which is a horror beyond words, but after death will come the Judgment—the ultimate out-of-the-frying-pan-into-the-fire experience. They will be torn from this painful, duck-filled nightmare and thrown into the fire of the just wrath of Almighty God.

This is why it is beneficial to tell sinners that death is an appointment. The Law shows how angry God is. It turns their laughter into mourning, and their joy into heaviness. It puts a weight on their shoulders that they cannot bear. When they feel the weight of their sins, their ear is primed to hear the words of the Savior: "Come to Me, all you who labor and are heavy laden, and I will give you rest" (Matthew 11:28).

In London, England, designers of a massive skyscraper made the mistake of using curved mirrored windows on their building. For two weeks each year, the concave design and mirrored glass of 20 Fenchurch Street reflects the sun off the windows and concentrates sunlight and heat on the road below. The temperature on the ground reaches up to 190 degrees Fahrenheit. Nearby shops and cars have been damaged by the intense sun rays. A shopkeeper had his doormat start smoking, another had blistered paint, and one journalist fried an egg with the rays.[15]

When we do what Jesus did in Mark 10:17 and concentrate the light of the Law on the conscience of the sinner, he feels the heat and sees his terrible danger.

Notice that Joseph "served" the prisoners (verse 4). This was a prison. Joseph, a prisoner, had been put in charge of other prisoners, yet he *served* them. So are we to humbly serve guilty sinners:

> And a servant of the Lord must not quarrel but be gentle to all, able to teach, patient, in humility correcting those who are in opposition, if God perhaps will grant them repentance, so that they may know the truth, and that they may come to their senses and escape the snare of the devil, having been taken captive by him to do his will. (2 Timothy 2:24–26)

We must never argue or become angry with the unsaved. If we do, our problem may be one of pride. Instead, we are to correct them in humility because we are no better than they are. They have been taken captive by the devil to do his will, and because they are prisoners compassion should fill our hearts and be evident in our words.

> Then the butler and the baker of the king of Egypt, who were confined in the prison, had a dream, both of them, each man's dream in one night and each man's dream with its own interpretation. And Joseph came in to them in the morning and looked at them, and saw that they were sad. So he asked Pharaoh's officers who were with him in the custody of his lord's house, saying, "Why do you look so sad today?" (Genesis 40:5–7)

God has given every human being a dream, and He has entrusted us to rightly interpret that dream. He has placed eternity in the hearts of humanity (Ecclesiastes 3:11). It is a distant echo of Eden, a shadow of immortality. We are not animals. We dream of something more than this painful existence—where day after day we are plagued with thieves of joy. No one makes it through life unscathed. No sinner dies without a cry that they might hold on to the precious life that is being ripped from their unwilling hands. And so, while they have life and breath, that nebulous dream drives billions to religiously search for immortality.

I received this email from a twenty-six-year-old woman who had been awakened by that dream:

> Growing up I kind of put God on the back burner. I would accept things that were told to me about God and Jesus but I never really applied them to my life much. I was too caught up in other things and I never really worried about death because I strangely felt like I was just invincible and nothing bad would happen to me. Now that I am an adult and I think more critically, I began to get extreme anxiety and fear that God isn't real. Now that I have realized my mortality, I am extremely afraid of death and where I will end up in the afterlife, which I have been questioning if there is one at this point... worried that what science says is true and we're all just an accident or we came from evolution...
>
> I then made a decision today and I repented to God asking Him for forgiveness telling Him how I am a sinner and I have gone against His Law. It's true, I am a lustful, lying thief and I have done other things as well. I thanked Jesus for dying on the cross and taking my sins upon Him so many years ago.

Joseph saw that his fellow prisoners were sad and asked, "Why do you look so sad today?" That is a strange question. *Why shouldn't they be sad?* They were in a cold dungeon. They had not only lost their positions in the palace, but had lost their freedom and were separated from their families. They *should* have been sad. But Joseph asked why they were sad "today." It clearly wasn't their environment that caused their sadness; it was the dream.

The whole world is tragically sad. We are sad when our childhood dog dies. We are sad when Grandpa dies. Memories of climbing up on his lap and feeling his hands lovingly run through our hair now become sad memories. Those recollections can become an overwhelming nostalgia. When Grandma dies, it adds to the pain. And as life unfolds, it does so like the layers of an onion. Tears color wherever you look because you see destruction, death, rape, murder, theft, suicide, greed, divorce, bitterness, bullying, racism, corruption, and a million and one other deadly ducks that wait in line to crush this whole sad world to death. Again, animals don't care about eternity; it's not written in their hearts. But we do, because were made in the image of God. We know that life is better than death. For the blind world, that uninterpreted dream of immortality makes death even more bitter.

When the baker and the butler said, "We each have had a dream, and there is no interpreter of it," Joseph had an answer. He said, "Do not interpretations belong to God? Tell them to me, please" (Genesis 40:8).

We say to a groping world that is suffocating in sadness and the haunting thoughts of death—*we have the answer!* Because we know God, we can interpret the mystery; we can tell them that they can know the truth and it shall make them free: "We can tell you why you have a fear of death and a cry for eternity in your hearts. God put it there, and He made a way for you to grasp it with both hands—it is through the glorious gospel of Jesus Christ."

And so the butler shares his mysterious dream:

> Then the chief butler told his dream to Joseph, and said to him, "Behold, in my dream a vine was before me, and in the vine were three branches; it was as though it budded, its blossoms shot forth, and its clusters brought forth ripe grapes. Then Pharaoh's cup was in my hand; and I took the

grapes and pressed them into Pharaoh's cup, and placed the cup in Pharaoh's hand." (Genesis 40:9–11)

A wise man once said that whenever you see the word "Behold" in Scripture, stop for a moment and consider what you're about to hear—because the word is a trumpet announcing important truths. Jesus often blew that trumpet. These words are a synopsis of the gospel. Jesus is the vine of which he spoke:

> "I am the vine, you are the branches. He who abides in Me, and I in him, bears much fruit; for without Me you can do nothing." (John 15:5)

Scripture likens His blood to wine:

> And as they were eating, Jesus took bread, blessed and broke it, and gave it to the disciples and said, "Take, eat; this is My body."
>
> Then He took the cup, and gave thanks, and gave it to them, saying, "Drink from it, all of you. For this is My blood of the new covenant, which is shed for many for the remission of sins. But I say to you, I will not drink of this fruit of the vine from now on until that day when I drink it new with you in My Father's kingdom." (Matthew 26:26–29)

It was on the cross that Jesus, the spotless Lamb of God, shed His precious blood for our sins. When our salvation was completed He cried, "It is finished," and dismissed His Spirit. Death then seized upon Him. But in three days, life came from the dead. It budded and blossomed through the glorious resurrection of the Son of God. It was impossible for death to hold Him.

It is through faith in the death and resurrection of Jesus Christ that guilty sinners are released from the prison of sin and death and find immortality:

"I am he that liveth, and was dead; and, behold, I am alive for evermore, Amen; and have the keys of hell and of death." (Revelation 1:18, KJV)

In Christ the mystery is solved; the dream of Eden is realized in the truth of Scripture. The eternity that was in our hearts becomes a promised reality. Look at these exceedingly great and precious promises:

> For I consider that the sufferings of this present time are not worthy to be compared with the glory which shall be revealed in us. For the earnest expectation of the creation eagerly waits for the revealing of the sons of God. For the creation was subjected to futility, not willingly, but because of Him who subjected it in hope; because the creation itself also will be delivered from the bondage of corruption into the glorious liberty of the children of God. (Romans 8:18–21)

The butler is symbolic of those who trust in the blood of Jesus and in His death and resurrection.

Like the butler, we will soon be out of this cold dungeon:

> And Joseph said to him, "This is the interpretation of it: The three branches are three days. Now within three days Pharaoh will lift up your head and restore you to your place, and you will put Pharaoh's cup in his hand according to the former manner, when you were his butler." (Genesis 40:12,13)

Then Joseph reveals his humanity. He has been horribly wronged and longs to be free from the confines of prison:

> "But remember me when it is well with you, and please show kindness to me; make mention of me to Pharaoh, and get me out of this house. For indeed I was stolen away from the land of the Hebrews; and also I have done noth-

ing here that they should put me into the dungeon."
(Genesis 40:14,15)

To the world, there are thousands of different religions
and the subject of which one is true is confusing. But we
know better. Religion breaks down into just two categories.
There are those who trust in God's mercy for salvation, and
those who trust in their own works as a means of obtaining
salvation.

The butler is symbolic of those who trust in the blood of
Jesus and in His death and resurrection. These are those the
Bible calls the "ransomed of the Lord":

> So the ransomed of the Lord shall return, and come to
> Zion with singing, with everlasting joy on their heads.
> They shall obtain joy and gladness; sorrow and sighing
> shall flee away. (Isaiah 51:11)

They are saved from the winepress of the wrath of Almighty God, because their sin debt has been paid by the sac-
rificial Lamb: "Jesus who delivers us from the wrath to come"
(1 Thessalonians 1:10). Death passes over those who have
applied His shed blood.

The baker, by contrast, is symbolic of those who trust in
their own works:

> When the chief baker saw that the interpretation was
> good, he said to Joseph, "I also was in my dream, and
> there were three white baskets on my head. In the upper-
> most basket were all kinds of baked goods for Pharaoh,
> and the birds ate them out of the basket on my head."
> (Genesis 40:16,17)

Those who trust in the work of their own hands as a
means of salvation don't believe they need the cleansing
blood. They don't need the white robes of salvation because
in their eyes, their good works are acceptable to their Cre-

ator. They have all kinds of baked goods for God. They give to the poor. They give to their church. They give themselves in good works, and the religious works of prayer, fasting, praise, and self-denial. But their works are demonic. "Birds" eat out of the basket that was on his head. Their offering basket is empty. When speaking of the sacrifice of "works" salvation, Scripture warns that "the things which the Gentiles sacrifice they sacrifice to demons and not to God, and I do not want you to have fellowship with demons" (1 Corinthians 10:20).

We are called, like Joseph, to faithfully give the world the interpretation of their dream of immortality.

Joseph then gives the interpretation of the baker's dream:

So Joseph answered and said, "This is the interpretation of it: The three baskets are three days. Within three days Pharaoh will lift off your head from you and hang you on a tree; and the birds will eat your flesh from you."

Now it came to pass on the third day, which was Pharaoh's birthday, that he made a feast for all his servants; and he lifted up the head of the chief butler and of the chief baker among his servants. Then he restored the chief butler to his butlership again, and he placed the cup in Pharaoh's hand. But he hanged the chief baker, as Joseph had interpreted to them. (Genesis 40:18–22)

Scripture doesn't tell us the crime of the chief baker. It must have been serious. Perhaps he tried to poison the Pharaoh. As the chief baker, he would have had opportunity to do so. Whatever the case, he was held in prison until he was executed.

I once heard a TV host say that he wouldn't be hosting the program the following week, because he was having a knee operation. Then he added something I'll never forget: "...which is no big deal—*if it's not your knee.*" That is so true. We rarely enter into empathy unless it's personalized.

It's the same with someone's death. We have a measure of sympathy when we hear of someone's passing. But when it comes to our *personal* death, it's so frightening it takes our breath away.

Did you ever think about the fact that each of us will die alone? We may have family there to comfort us, but that's only while we're alive. The moment we die we will leave them, and we will leave *alone.* As a Christian, I came into this world with nothing, but I will leave with my hand in the hand of Jesus. That is my comfort, and yet at the same time I'm horrified by the thought of anyone dying alone.

We are called, like Joseph, to faithfully give the world the interpretation of their dream of immortality. The "interpretation" comes through the gospel. It shows them that they need to forsake their futile efforts of religion. God will not be bribed to turn a blind eye to sin. If they persist in their self-righteousness, God will carry out perfect justice on the Day of Wrath, and that will be a terrifying thing. Paul said,

> Knowing, therefore, the terror of the Lord, we persuade men... (2 Corinthians 5:11)

We are to tell them to trust only in the shed blood of Jesus.

> Yet the chief butler did not remember Joseph, but forgot him. (Genesis 40:23)

Ingratitude is a horrible sin. Joseph was forgotten by the butler. How could that happen? Joseph interpreted the dreams correctly, and in doing so, he demonstrated that he had a special relationship with the Living God.

How could anyone who professes to have been freed from sin and death by Jesus Christ forget Him? Yet many do. They, like the nine ungrateful lepers, were cleansed, and go their way without a heart of thanks. Only one came back and fell at His feet in gratitude (Luke 17:12–15). Have we done that? Have you and I fallen at the precious feet of the Savior, and then been set ablaze to tell a dying world of Him and His cross? I hope so.

Questions

1. Explain how the narrative of the butler and the baker are two pictures of salvation.

2. What was it that convinced them that the Pharaoh was angry with them?

3. Why is humanity tragically "sad"?

4. With what do we address that sadness?

5. How can you and I best express gratitude to God for our cleansing of sin?

Chapter Eleven

TWO FULL YEARS

In the following passage of Scripture we are told that Joseph waited "two full years." The word "full" is telling. If you want time to drag, wait for something. Wait for a dentist to get back to you as you sit with a mouthful of weird stuff in his chair. Wait in a crowded airport for a delayed flight. Or wait in a stinking and lonely dungeon for a butler to remember that you had done him a favor. The days must have been long.

> Then it came to pass, at the end of two full years, that Pharaoh had a dream; and behold, he stood by the river. Suddenly there came up out of the river seven cows, fine looking and fat; and they fed in the meadow. Then behold, seven other cows came up after them out of the river, ugly and gaunt, and stood by the other cows on the bank of the river. And the ugly and gaunt cows ate up the seven fine looking and fat cows. So Pharaoh awoke. (Genesis 41:1–4)

The God who created lightning sometimes seems to move at a snail's pace. I'm sure that a hope of release from prison came to Joseph when God gave him the interpretation for both the baker's and butler's dreams. Knowing that he heard from the Lord meant God knew about his hopeless situation. Surely the butler would be grateful and immediately intercede for him with Pharaoh for the equivalent of a presidential pardon. But day after day dragged by for another two full years, and "hope deferred makes the heart sick" (Proverbs 13:12).

But God was still into giving dreams. Unbeknown to Joseph, He was spooking Pharaoh with thin cannibal cows that couldn't resist the taste of beef. Seven fat cows came up out of the river, followed by seven thin cows that also came up out of the river. The latter stood there on the bank for a moment, had some sort of beef with their own kind, and ate them. The Scriptures then say, "So Pharaoh awoke." It's a relief to wake up from weird dreams. Perhaps he wondered if it was something he'd eaten before he went to bed. Maybe it was the beef kebabs. No doubt he dismissed it as just another weird, meaningless dream. Sometimes we tell friends and family about strange dreams, but this one was staying under his pillow; it was too weird. But then something even stranger happened:

Stalks of grain may have heads, but they don't have mouths. Yet they were cereal killers; they ate each other.

> He slept and dreamed a second time; and suddenly seven heads of grain came up on one stalk, plump and good. Then behold, seven thin heads, blighted by the east wind, sprang up after them. And the seven thin heads devoured the seven plump and full heads. So Pharaoh awoke, and

indeed, it was a dream. Now it came to pass in the morning that his spirit was troubled, and he sent and called for all the magicians of Egypt and all its wise men. And Pharaoh told them his dreams, but there was no one who could interpret them for Pharaoh. (Genesis 41:5–8)

This probably doesn't need pointing out: stalks of grain may have heads, but they don't have mouths. Yet they were cereal killers; they ate each other. This was a rerun of the cow dream. It was the same script, but with different actors. The fat cows had been replaced by fat grain. The grain appeared in teams of seven, just like the cows, and the thin grain ate the plump grain. We usually quickly forget crazy dreams, but this one also stayed with Pharaoh after he woke.

This dream was more than strange. It was troubling. So troubling that Pharaoh wasn't embarrassed to tell all, even though it might raise a few eyebrows.

Then the chief butler spoke to Pharaoh, saying: "I remember my faults this day. When Pharaoh was angry with his servants, and put me in custody in the house of the captain of the guard, both me and the chief baker, we each had a dream in one night, he and I. Each of us dreamed according to the interpretation of his own dream. Now there was a young Hebrew man with us there, a servant of the captain of the guard. And we told him, and he interpreted our dreams for us; to each man he interpreted according to his own dream. And it came to pass, just as he interpreted for us, so it happened. He restored me to my office, and he hanged him." (Genesis 41:9–13)

It took two full years for the sleeping butler to wake up to his faults. Pharaoh's dream reminded him of his own dream and the dream of his departed coworker, and that reminded him of his obligation to intercede for Joseph, as he had been asked to do.

Jesus has asked you and me to intercede with God for help to reach those who are held captive in the prison of sin:

> Then He said to His disciples, "The harvest truly is plentiful, but the laborers are few. Therefore pray the Lord of the harvest to send out laborers into His harvest." (Matthew 9:37,38)

Are you a disciple of Christ? Are you doing what He told you to do? Are you pleading with the Father to send out laborers for the unsaved, because you too were once held captive by sin and death? Or have you become too busy with your Christian life, and you have neglected your obligation to intercede?

The butler spoke up for Joseph, and that meant Joseph's time of trial was finally over! The Pharaoh called for him, and he was quickly brought out of the prison and presented to Pharaoh:

> Then Pharaoh sent and called Joseph, and they brought him quickly out of the dungeon; and he shaved, changed his clothing, and came to Pharaoh. And Pharaoh said to Joseph, "I have had a dream, and there is no one who can interpret it. But I have heard it said of you that you can understand a dream, to interpret it." So Joseph answered Pharaoh, saying, "It is not in me; God will give Pharaoh an answer of peace." (Genesis 41:14–16)

This is the key to Joseph's walk with God. He not only had a humble heart, he had faith in his Maker. He was prepared to go out on a limb and trust the Lord to once again give him the interpretation.

Humility of heart and faith in God are the keys to the Christian life. Pride is such a lie. What do we have that we haven't received? Only our sin. Every atom of ability we have comes from God. Without Him we can do nothing.

It was then that Pharaoh was emboldened to relate his dream in even more detail:

> Then Pharaoh said to Joseph: "Behold, in my dream I stood on the bank of the river. Suddenly seven cows came up out of the river, fine looking and fat; and they fed in the meadow. Then behold, seven other cows came up after them, poor and very ugly and gaunt, such ugliness as I have never seen in all the land of Egypt. And the gaunt and ugly cows ate up the first seven, the fat cows. When they had eaten them up, no one would have known that they had eaten them, for they were just as ugly as at the beginning. So I awoke. Also I saw in my dream, and suddenly seven heads came up on one stalk, full and good. Then behold, seven heads, withered, thin, and blighted by the east wind, sprang up after them. And the thin heads devoured the seven good heads. So I told this to the magicians, but there was no one who could explain it to me." (Genesis 41:17–24)

Without God the world can't solve the mystery of life. Its interpretation is hidden from them. Albert Einstein said,

> What is the meaning of human life, or of organic life altogether? To answer this question at all implies a religion. Is there any sense then, you ask, in putting it? I answer, the man who regards his own life and that of his fellow creatures as meaningless is not merely unfortunate but almost disqualified for life.[16]

Without God nothing makes sense. Our existence has no rhyme or reason. Life is futile and hopeless, and in the face of impending death, we are helpless.

> Then Joseph said to Pharaoh, "The dreams of Pharaoh are one; God has shown Pharaoh what He is about to do…" (Genesis 41:25)

Joseph was the experienced dream-whisperer. Many years earlier he too had two dreams that were one, in which God had shown him what He was going to do. Joseph dreamed that his brothers' sheaves stood all around and bowed down to his sheaf. Then he dreamed another dream, this time that the sun, the moon, and the eleven stars bowed down to him (see Genesis 37:7–9). Both dreams were one—just like Pharaoh's dreams.

Joseph then told Pharaoh his future. This was no generic fortune cookie; it was very detailed and specific as to what he was to do. Egypt would have seven years of great prosperity followed by seven years of terrible famine. God was telling Pharaoh not to be irresponsible when things were humming, but to prepare for the coming days.

Whatever the future has for us, we need to store up the grain of His Word in our hearts for times of famine.

Only our omniscient God knows the future. Man makes out that he does, with endless political pundits who take polls, weather forecasters who review computer data and help us plan trips to Disneyland, and fortunetellers who make their fortunes by ripping off the simple. But only God knows what tomorrow will bring—and He has a proven track record in His Word. Whatever the future has for us, we need to store up the grain of His Word in our hearts for times of famine.

It was now time for the purposes of God to be realized in the life of this emancipated slave:

> So the advice was good in the eyes of Pharaoh and in the eyes of all his servants. And Pharaoh said to his servants, "Can we find such a one as this, a man in whom is the Spirit of God?" Then Pharaoh said to Joseph, "Inasmuch

as God has shown you all this, there is no one as discerning and wise as you. You shall be over my house, and all my people shall be ruled according to your word; only in regard to the throne will I be greater than you." And Pharaoh said to Joseph, "See, I have set you over all the land of Egypt."

Then Pharaoh took his signet ring off his hand and put it on Joseph's hand; and he clothed him in garments of fine linen and put a gold chain around his neck. And he had him ride in the second chariot which he had; and they cried out before him, "Bow the knee!" So he set him over all the land of Egypt. (Genesis 41:37–42)

We are also told when Joseph's ministry of deliverance began:

Joseph was thirty years old when he stood before Pharaoh king of Egypt. And Joseph went out from the presence of Pharaoh, and went throughout all the land of Egypt. (verse 46)

Now Jesus Himself began His ministry at about thirty years of age, being (as was supposed) the son of Joseph, the son of Heli… (Luke 3:23)

Jesus was made a little lower than the angels for the suffering of death, that He might taste death for everyone. And now God has highly exalted Him, giving Him a name that is above every name, that at the name of Jesus every knee should bow in Heaven and on earth. He has given Him all authority in Heaven and on earth, clothing Him in the fine linen of perfect righteousness, glorified forever, exalting Him to His right hand to rule and reign forever.

Questions

1. Do you sometimes feel that God is slow in answering your prayers? Give some examples.

2. Have you ever been asked by someone to pray about something, and you forgot? How did this make you feel?

3. How often do you pray for the Lord of the harvest to send laborers into the harvest fields?

4. What are two major keys to the Christian life?

5. Have you found that there are other keys to help your growth in Christ? What are they?

Chapter Twelve

THERE IS GRAIN IN EGYPT

The famine that Joseph had warned Pharaoh about had arrived in the region. Joseph's family in Canaan was facing starvation, while Egypt had become a land of plenty.

> When Jacob saw that there was grain in Egypt, Jacob said to his sons, "Why do you look at one another?" And he said, "Indeed I have heard that there is grain in Egypt; go down to that place and buy for us there, that we may live and not die." (Genesis 42:1,2)

Grain meant bread for Jacob and his family, and bread meant more than food. It meant life rather than death by starvation. The food shortage was deadly serious.

The situation for all of humanity is equally serious—more serious than a heart attack. Everyone is dying for lack of the Bread of Life. It's just a matter of time. Jesus is the source of life, and without Him sinners will perish. So why are they standing around looking at one another? They are starving to death! Why aren't they crying out to God to save them?

> Why do you spend money for what is not bread,
> And your wages for what does not satisfy?
> Listen carefully to Me, and eat what is good,
> And let your soul delight itself in abundance. (Isaiah 55:2)

Joseph's brothers took their father's word to heart. They didn't stand around looking at each other but went in search of life-sustaining food:

> So Joseph's ten brothers went down to buy grain in Egypt. But Jacob did not send Joseph's brother Benjamin with his brothers, for he said, "Lest some calamity befall him." And the sons of Israel went to buy grain among those who journeyed, for the famine was in the land of Canaan.
>
> Now Joseph was governor over the land; and it was he who sold to all the people of the land. And Joseph's brothers came and bowed down before him with their faces to the earth. (Genesis 42:3–6)

Like Joseph's ten brothers, the Ten Commandments bring us to the Bread of Life. Scripture says that the moral Law is a "tutor" to bring us to Christ (see Galatians 3:24). The Law prepares our hearts for grace. The Ten Commandments bow in submission before the face of the Savior. How could they not? They issue from His nature.

God loves His Law. He loves righteousness, justice, and truth, and the Day will come when Eternal Justice has its way. Adolf Hitler escaped the wrath of the Russians with a quick bullet to the head, but he won't escape the wrath of God.

When we open up each Commandment as we speak to an unsaved person, we have one eye on the cross. We are praying that his conscience will do its God-given duty and accuse him of sin (see Romans 2:15). This is because it is the knowledge of sin that shows us our need of the Savior.

> Joseph saw his brothers and recognized them, but he acted
> as a stranger to them and spoke roughly to them. Then he
> said to them, "Where do you come from?"
>> And they said, "From the land of Canaan to buy food."
>> So Joseph recognized his brothers, but they did not
> recognize him. (verses 7,8)

Joseph was looking for contrition. He was longing to
reveal himself to them, but he dare not if murder still lurked
in their hearts.

How we long to reveal Jesus to this
blind world. They don't know who He
is. They think He was just a religious
teacher or a great man. They don't know
that in Christ we have treasure in earth-
en vessels. We have Christ in us, the
hope of glory. God has sealed us in Him
with the gift of everlasting life.

Like Joseph's

ten brothers,

the Ten

Commandments

bring us to the

Bread of Life.

Nor will the lost know who He is if
they don't come with a broken spirit, a
contrite heart, and a bowed knee. And so we hold back from
preaching Jesus until the Law has done its work. It must prepare the soil for the seed of the Word of God, and until there
is understanding, the preaching of the cross will remain foolishness.

> Then Joseph remembered the dreams which he had
> dreamed about them, and said to them, "You are spies!
> You have come to see the nakedness of the land!" (verse 9)

And so begin the words of Joseph that were designed to
put the fear of God in the heart of his brothers. There is a
fear that is both good and necessary for salvation. The
Scriptures tell us that through the fear of the Lord men de-
part from evil (see Proverbs 16:6). Without a healthy fear of

God, sinners don't feel compelled to let go of their beloved sin.

How the words of Jesus accuse and terrify us until we find shelter in the cross. "Whoever looks at a woman to lust for her" (Matthew 5:28) thrust into my sinful heart like a burning arrow before I came to Christ. Jesus magnified the Law and made it honorable. As the Law increased, I deceased in my own eyes. As it was made honorable, I was dishonored by the knowledge of my sinful heart. It reduced me to nothing. It ripped away my fig leaves, humbled me, and left me helpless and hopeless—stopping my mouth and leaving me without justification before a holy Judge (see Romans 3:19,20).

> And they said to him, "No, my lord, but your servants have come to buy food. We are all one man's sons; we are honest men; your servants are not spies." (verses 10,11)

They claimed that they were honest men, when they were not. They were wicked and hateful men who had attempted to murder their own brother, sold him into slavery, and had horribly lied to and dishonored their own father.

When the Law in the hand of the Holy Spirit first sheds light on the sinful heart, it causes men to try to justify themselves. Like the rich young ruler, they typically say, "But I'm a good person. I have weaknesses like everyone else, but those were just white lies and little things I took... and I did those things in the past. They were mistakes—learning lessons." They trivialize their crimes against God and in doing so, show that they don't yet have contrition. Watch Jesus use the moral Law to bring the knowledge of sin:

> Now as He was going out on the road, one came running, knelt before Him, and asked Him, "Good Teacher, what shall I do that I may inherit eternal life?"

So Jesus said to him, "Why do you call Me good? No one is good but One, that is, God. You know the commandments: 'Do not commit adultery,' 'Do not murder,' 'Do not steal,' 'Do not bear false witness,' 'Do not defraud,' 'Honor your father and your mother.'"

And he answered and said to Him, "Teacher, all these things I have kept from my youth."

Then Jesus, looking at him, loved him, and said to him, "One thing you lack: Go your way, sell whatever you have and give to the poor, and you will have treasure in heaven; and come, take up the cross, and follow Me."

But he was sad at this word, and went away sorrowful, for he had great possessions. (Mark 10:17–22)

This man seemed to be sincere, humble, and earnest. He ran to Jesus. There was a sense of urgency. Perhaps he had had the revelation that death could sweep him into eternity in a heartbeat. Perhaps he had just lost a loved one and had been reminded of his own appointment with the Grim Reaper. Whatever the case, he ran to Jesus. And he knelt before Him; he showed respect and humility. Then he complimented Jesus by calling Him "good." One would think that this was a prime candidate for the gospel. But he wasn't. He wasn't like Nicodemus who came by night to the Savior (see John 3). Jesus gave him the gospel. But He didn't give the good news of free salvation to this rich young ruler, because the man was self-righteous.

How do you react when some calls you a "good" Christian? I tell them I'm not good. I'm a wretched sinner, saved only by the mercy of God. Like Paul, I say that in me dwells no good thing (see Romans 7:18). When the Bible speaks of "good," it means moral perfection, in thought, word, and deed. Only God is good, and it's only by seeing His moral perfection that we can see our own sin.

Joseph terrorized his guilty brothers. He brought them to a place of despair, and his words began to expose a measure of the truth. They mentioned their lost brother: "...and one is no more":

> But he said to them, "No, but you have come to see the nakedness of the land."
>
> And they said, "Your servants are twelve brothers, the sons of one man in the land of Canaan; and in fact, the youngest is with our father today, and one is no more."
>
> But Joseph said to them, "It is as I spoke to you, saying, 'You are spies!' In this manner you shall be tested: By the life of Pharaoh, you shall not leave this place unless your youngest brother comes here. Send one of you, and let him bring your brother; and you shall be kept in prison, that your words may be tested to see whether there is any truth in you; or else, by the life of Pharaoh, surely you are spies!" So he put them all together in prison three days. (Genesis 42:12–17)

The Law searches us out. It demands truth in the inward parts, and when it spies guilt, it puts us in prison:

> But before faith came, we were kept under guard by the law, kept for the faith which would afterward be revealed. Therefore the law was our tutor to bring us to Christ, that we might be justified by faith. (Galatians 3:23,24)

However, Joseph's desire wasn't to condemn his brothers. He loved them and wanted to bring them into a land of abundance. And so our objective in bringing the burden of the Law to sinners is to prepare their heart for the message of God's grace. We want to bring them to Christ where they will be justified by faith and find entrance into the Kingdom of God.

How thorough and faithful we must be to use the Law when we speak to the lost. Too many give the good news, pray a "sinner's prayer," and think that they have sealed the deal. In truth they have done nothing but produce a false convert—one who names the name of Christ but hasn't departed from iniquity.

> Then Joseph said to them the third day, "Do this and live, for I fear God: If you are honest men, let one of your brothers be confined to your prison house; but you, go and carry grain for the famine of your houses. And bring your youngest brother to me; so your words will be verified, and you shall not die." And they did so. (Genesis 42:18–20)

Joseph wanted their most precious possession. He wanted their youngest brother. They knew how much their father loved Benjamin and what it would mean to take this son from him. It brought back the memory of another they had ripped from his hands:

> Then they said to one another, "We are truly guilty concerning our brother, for we saw the anguish of his soul when he pleaded with us, and we would not hear; therefore this distress has come upon us."
>
> And Reuben answered them, saying, "Did I not speak to you, saying, 'Do not sin against the boy'; and you would not listen? Therefore behold, his blood is now required of us." But they did not know that Joseph understood them, for he spoke to them through an interpreter. And he turned himself away from them and wept. Then he returned to them again, and talked with them. And he took Simeon from them and bound him before their eyes. (verses 21–24)

The Law reminds us of past sins. It searches the corridors of the heart and brings to remembrance secret sins. It points the finger at David and accuses of sin. It shows the supposed sincere, humble, and earnest rich young ruler that he loved

his money more than he loved the God who gave him life
and the wealth he loved.

> Then Joseph gave a command to fill their sacks with grain,
> to restore every man's money to his sack, and to give them
> provisions for the journey. Thus he did for them. (verse 25)

The brothers thought that they would simply go to Egypt
and buy grain. Once they had the grain their problem was
solved. They would live.

The sinner knows that he has a problem with God, but
thinks if he has sinned, it is a simple matter of balancing the
scales. Good works will fix everything. But God rejects any
attempts to purchase everlasting life. Good works cannot
buy salvation from death. There is a way that seems right,
but for sinners who come thinking they can purchase salvation, it is a dead-end street. God will not be bribed to turn a
blind eye to their sin.

> So they loaded their donkeys with the grain and departed
> from there. But as one of them opened his sack to give his
> donkey feed at the encampment, he saw his money; and
> there it was, in the mouth of his sack. So he said to his
> brothers, "My money has been restored, and there it is, in
> my sack!" Then their hearts failed them and they were
> afraid, saying to one another, "What is this that God has
> done to us?" (verses 26–28)

Joseph didn't want their money; he wanted their love.
The money was therefore returned.

It is a wonderful revelation for the lost to find out that
God will not be bought off by good works. It is bad news but
a huge blessing in disguise. Those who trust in good works
never know if they have done enough to balance the scales.
They pass into death with a false hope. But learning that our
"good" works are an abomination to God is the first step

toward the relief of God's amazing grace, as John Newton noted:

'Twas grace that taught my heart to fear,
And grace my fears relieved;
How precious did that grace appear
The hour I first believed!

Seeing his sins causes the sinner's heart to fail and he becomes afraid. For the first time in his godless life, he no longer sees God as being congenial. His smile turns to a frown as he realizes the truth about his hopeless condition.

> Then they went to Jacob their father in the land of Canaan and told him all that had happened to them, saying: "The man who is lord of the land spoke roughly to us, and took us for spies of the country. But we said to him, 'We are honest men; we are not spies. We are twelve brothers, sons of our father; one is no more, and the youngest is with our father this day in the land of Canaan.' Then the man, the lord of the country, said to us, 'By this I will know that you are honest men: Leave one of your brothers here with me, take food for the famine of your households, and be gone. And bring your youngest brother to me; so I shall know that you are not spies, but that you are honest men. I will grant your brother to you, and you may trade in the land.'"
>
> Then it happened as they emptied their sacks, that surprisingly each man's bundle of money was in his sack; and when they and their father saw the bundles of money, they were afraid. (verses 29–35)

All humanity is shut up under the Law. There isn't a righteous person on the face of this earth. No matter how good, kind, giving, and religious, no one is going to be justified by works. From Cain who came with grain in his hand, to the Pharisees, to the billions whose hope is in a religion of good works, no one will succeed in bribing the Judge of the Universe: "The sacrifice of the wicked is an abomination to the LORD" (Proverbs 15:8).

> And Jacob their father said to them, "You have bereaved me: Joseph is no more, Simeon is no more, and you want to take Benjamin. All these things are against me."
>
> Then Reuben spoke to his father, saying, "Kill my two sons if I do not bring him back to you; put him in my hands, and I will bring him back to you."
>
> But he said, "My son shall not go down with you, for his brother is dead, and he is left alone. If any calamity should befall him along the way in which you go, then you would bring down my gray hair with sorrow to the grave." (verses 36–38)

Reuben was quick to offer the lives of his two sons. I'm not sure how his sons felt about that. No doubt he was just trying to impress upon his father that there was no way he would return without Benjamin, and this was his way of expressing it. But it wasn't Reuben who changed Jacob's mind about letting them take his beloved son. It was something else, as we will see in the next chapter.

Questions

1. Why didn't Jacob want Benjamin to go to Egypt?

2. Explain the biblical function of the Ten Commandments.

3. What was it that Joseph was looking for in his brothers, and why is it so important in a sinner who comes to the Savior?

4. Quote some of the things Jesus said that put the fear of God in guilty sinners.

5. Why aren't good works acceptable to God as a means of salvation?

Chapter Thirteen

NO DEAL WITHOUT BENJAMIN

Joseph's brothers were now back in their homeland. For Jacob, the option of them returning to Egypt with Benjamin was out of the question. It was not negotiable—not even with Reuben's over-the-top assurance that all would be well. It wasn't even on the table.

> Now the famine was severe in the land. And it came to pass, when they had eaten up the grain which they had brought from Egypt, that their father said to them, "Go back, buy us a little food."
>
> But Judah spoke to him, saying, "The man solemnly warned us, saying, 'You shall not see my face unless your brother is with you.' If you send our brother with us, we will go down and buy you food. But if you will not send him, we will not go down; for the man said to us, 'You shall not see my face unless your brother is with you.'"
>
> And Israel said, "Why did you deal so wrongfully with me as to tell the man whether you had still another brother?" (Genesis 43:1–6).

We don't truly appreciate God's hand in providing daily bread until we grow hungry. The famine was severe in Israel—severe enough to change Jacob's mind about his sons returning to Egypt. He told them to go back and buy a "little" food. Judah knew that the conditions placed on purchasing food were not negotiable. No brother, no food. But his father didn't take to heart what they had been told by "the man." Surely they could buy a small quantity of food, he thought.

Sin can't be that serious. But it is, and the Lord of lords says that we must bring our brother.

Before we come to Christ, we are each famished for life. Every one of us is dying, and God is the only One who can save us from death. The ungodly want to hold onto their good works. Surely God will let them into Heaven; sin can't be that serious. But it is, and the Lord of lords says that we must bring our brother.

Three times in the New Testament, Jesus is referred to as our brother:

And He looked around in a circle at those who sat about Him, and said, "Here are My mother and My brothers!" (Mark 3:34)

For whom He foreknew, He also predestined to be conformed to the image of His Son, that He might be the firstborn among many brethren. (Romans 8:29)

For both He who sanctifies and those who are being sanctified are all of one, for which reason He is not ashamed to call them brethren. (Hebrews 2:11)

Jacob had a false hope. His sons knew that there was no hope of food unless they met the man's condition. They pointed to Benjamin as the only hope. And so the Commandments cannot do anything but point us to Jesus. Again, the Law is our tutor to bring us to Christ (see Galatians 3:24).

We cannot negotiate with God without the Savior. Jesus is the only Mediator between God and men, and no one comes to the Father but by Him (see 1 Timothy 2:5; John 14:6). Sinners think that God will make an exception in their case; they think that they are going to get into Heaven without the Savior. But salvation without the shed blood of the Lamb is not negotiable. It's not even on the table.

> But they said, "The man asked us pointedly about ourselves and our family, saying, 'Is your father still alive? Have you another brother?' And we told him according to these words. Could we possibly have known that he would say, 'Bring your brother down'?"
>
> Then Judah said to Israel his father, "Send the lad with me, and we will arise and go, that we may live and not die, both we and you and also our little ones. I myself will be surety for him; from my hand you shall require him. If I do not bring him back to you and set him before you, then let me bear the blame forever. For if we had not lingered, surely by now we would have returned this second time." (Genesis 43:7–10)

Joseph, in demanding that his brothers bring back Benjamin, was testing their sincerity. Would they take lightly the thought of hurting their father once again? Their jealousy had ripped the joy he had in Joseph from his hands. Could they do it with Benjamin? Or was theirs a regret that would lead to godly sorrow—a sorrow that produces repentance?

All this was happening to fulfill the mind-boggling purposes of God. How could He have orchestrated such a scenario with Joseph's father and brothers? How could He have seen the future, knowing that Joseph's hateful brothers would one day bow down to him?

And how could our Creator not only know about each of us, but be so intimately familiar with us that He knows how many hairs are on our heads (see Luke 12:7)? And even more mind-blowing is that He is orchestrating circumstances in our lives to fulfill His purposes. Why would we then linger? Why would we not devour His precious Word daily, seek Him earnestly in prayer, crave His wisdom, worship His holy name, and preach His Word with passion to the perishing? What would hold us back? The answer is abundance. But when there is famine in the land, we are driven to our knees.

> And their father Israel said to them, "If it must be so, then do this: Take some of the best fruits of the land in your vessels and carry down a present for the man—a little balm and a little honey, spices and myrrh, pistachio nuts and almonds. Take double money in your hand, and take back in your hand the money that was returned in the mouth of your sacks; perhaps it was an oversight. Take your brother also, and arise, go back to the man. And may God Almighty give you mercy before the man, that he may release your other brother and Benjamin. If I am bereaved, I am bereaved!" (Genesis 43:11–14)

Famine made Jacob loosen his grip on Benjamin. It is wise for us to hold onto loved ones with a loose hand. We may think they are ours, but they really belong to God. He loaned you your children. He loaned you your spouse. For of Him and through Him and to Him are all things (see Romans 11:36). We don't draw a breath without His permissive will. He is our Creator, and the Creator of our beloved family, and life's circumstances can take them away from us. So make Him your first love. Make Him and His teachings your foundation. Strengthen your resolve to love Him with all of your heart, soul, mind, and strength. He will never leave you nor forsake you. Nothing can come between you and Him, not even death. This is all part of building your house on the rock, so that when the storms of life come you won't crumble.

> So the men took that present and Benjamin, and they took double money in their hand, and arose and went down to Egypt; and they stood before Joseph. When Joseph saw Benjamin with them, he said to the steward of his house, "Take these men to my home, and slaughter an animal and make ready; for these men will dine with me at noon." Then the man did as Joseph ordered, and the man brought the men into Joseph's house. (verses 15–17)

They took gifts with Benjamin. Likewise, our good works are acceptable to God when we present them in Christ (see Ephesians 2:10). They are the result of our gratitude for our salvation. This is because, to the redeemed, God is no longer our Judge. He is rather "Abba, Father," whose knee we may come and sit upon as His beloved child. We can even anticipate His praise for our works: "Well done, good and faithful servant" (Matthew 25:21).

> Now the men were afraid because they were brought into Joseph's house; and they said, "It is because of the money, which was returned in our sacks the first time, that we are brought in, so that he may make a case against us and seize us, to take us as slaves with our donkeys." (Genesis 43:18)

I wonder if such a scenario (of being seized against their will and made slaves) reminded them of their merciless betrayal of their own brother? I wonder if they had tried to justify what they had done to him, and the reality of their own enslavement birthed an empathy that was producing repentance?

It's when the thief puts himself in the place of those from whom he stole, or the rapist puts himself in the place of the person he violated, that hard impenitent hearts are softened. I wonder if Saul of Tarsus thought about Stephen's suffering, during those three days he lost his sight after the Damascus Road experience? And of course, our own hard hearts are softened by the sight of the Savior impaled on the cruel cross because of our sins.

> When they drew near to the steward of Joseph's house, they talked with him at the door of the house, and said, "O sir, we indeed came down the first time to buy food; but it happened, when we came to the encampment, that we opened our sacks, and there, each man's money was in the mouth of his sack, our money in full weight; so we have brought it back in our hand. And we have brought down other money in our hands to buy food. We do not know who put our money in our sacks."
>
> But he said, "Peace be with you, do not be afraid. Your God and the God of your father has given you treasure in your sacks; I had your money." Then he brought Simeon out to them.
>
> So the man brought the men into Joseph's house and gave them water, and they washed their feet; and he gave their donkeys feed. Then they made the present ready for Joseph's coming at noon, for they heard that they would eat bread there.
>
> And when Joseph came home, they brought him the present which was in their hand into the house, and bowed down before him to the earth. Then he asked them about their well-being, and said, "Is your father well, the old man of whom you spoke? Is he still alive?"
>
> And they answered, "Your servant our father is in good health; he is still alive." And they bowed their heads down and prostrated themselves. (verses 19–28)

Didn't the brothers put two and two together? Surely this was their brother Joseph. But they didn't recognize him from

the seventeen-year-old dreamer they had sold to the Ishmaelites. It was thirteen years later and his physical appearance may have changed. He was now a mature man, dressed
in fine Egyptian linen, not in his colorful shepherd's coat.
Besides, he spoke in another language and through an interpreter. They couldn't in their wildest dreams have known
that their maddening younger brother had not only become
Lord of Egypt, but held their very lives in the balance. And so
they fulfilled Joseph's dreams by prostrating themselves
before him.

Why doesn't the world put two and two together? Jesus
Christ is God. He is the Word become flesh. He is the express
image of the invisible God. He came to His own and they
didn't receive Him. Sinners don't know that this is the Christ,
the Son of the Living God. Their eyes are withheld from
knowing Him. The unsaved world has its own image of Jesus
of Nazareth, thinking He was just a man with some good
teachings on kindness and forgiveness, but that's all. They don't
know who He is because He speaks in another language:

> These things we also speak, not in words which man's wis-
> dom teaches but which the Holy Spirit teaches, comparing
> spiritual things with spiritual. But the natural man does
> not receive the things of the Spirit of God, for they are
> foolishness to him; nor can he know them, because they
> are spiritually discerned. (1 Corinthians 2:13,14)

Not in their wildest dreams would this blasphemous,
Christ-hating, and sin-loving world ever believe that they
will stand before Jesus as their God and Judge. And He will
determine their eternity:

> "When the Son of Man comes in His glory, and all the
> holy angels with Him, then He will sit on the throne of
> His glory. All the nations will be gathered before Him, and

He will separate them one from another, as a shepherd divides his sheep from the goats. And He will set the sheep on His right hand, but the goats on the left. Then the King will say to those on His right hand, 'Come, you blessed of My Father, inherit the kingdom prepared for you from the foundation of the world.'" (Matthew 25:31–34)

Words fail me to express my fear for those who will face this terrifying Day.

Then he lifted his eyes and saw his brother Benjamin, his mother's son, and said, "Is this your younger brother of whom you spoke to me?" And he said, "God be gracious to you, my son." Now his heart yearned for his brother; so Joseph made haste and sought somewhere to weep. And he went into his chamber and wept there. Then he washed his face and came out; and he restrained himself, and said, "Serve the bread."

So they set him a place by himself, and them by themselves, and the Egyptians who ate with him by themselves; because the Egyptians could not eat food with the Hebrews, for that is an abomination to the Egyptians. And they sat before him, the firstborn according to his birthright and the youngest according to his youth; and the men looked in astonishment at one another. Then he took servings to them from before him, but Benjamin's serving was five times as much as any of theirs. So they drank and were merry with him. (Genesis 43:29–34)

Think of what Joseph was doing. He was blatantly favoring Benjamin in front of his brothers, giving him five times their serving. They had one turkey leg, he had five. They had two roast potatoes, forget the carbohydrates, he had ten. If they had three exotic fruits in a bowl before them, he had fifteen. Was there any spark of jealousy in their hearts? Would they become inflamed with a burning hatred for Benjamin as they did with Joseph thirteen years earlier? But they were free of jealousy because they loved Benjamin. Love is never jealous or proud, or selfish or rude. It rejoices in the truth.

WHERE ARE THE MILLIONS?

Love also cares about the unsaved world. It is a friend of sinners, and goes out of its way to speak to an adulterous woman at the well.

Sam and I were on my bike looking for someone who would listen to the gospel. I prayed that God would lead me to somebody, but after a few minutes of riding I mumbled something about there being millions of people in America. Then I said, "Where is everyone?" Within about ten seconds I rounded a corner and saw a lone figure sitting in the bleachers opposite a baseball field. He was reading a book and had earbuds in his ears.

I stopped the bike and said loudly, "Did I give you one of these?" He pulled out an earbud, leaned forward over about four bleachers, and took a Ten Commandments coin. I then told him what it was and asked if he thought there was an afterlife. He wasn't sure, but said he thought about it all the time. When I asked him to come on camera, he declined, saying that he was too shy. I asked for his name and then I asked Ricardo if I could speak to him for a few moments. He was a little hesitant, so I asked him what he was reading. It was a book on Buddhism. So I said, "You are obviously searching, so let me speak to you for a few moments."

I said that I wanted to know if he thought he was a good person, and if he would therefore make it to Heaven. He said that he was, and so we went through the Commandments. I then shared the gospel, gave him a Subway gift card, signed a book for him, and pleaded with him to consider what we talked about.

As we rode off, I prayed for Ricardo—that he would read his Bible (he said he had two at home).

There are hundreds of millions of people in America, and yet God was interested in one person—as Jesus was with the woman at the well, and God was with one young man named Joseph. He was also interested in his brothers, whose dream was about to turn into a nightmare.

Questions

1. What was it that changed Jacob's mind about allowing Benjamin to go to Egypt?

2. What is the sinner's false hope?

3. What are some things you can do to ensure that your "house" won't crumble when the storms of life come?

4. Why are a Christian's good works acceptable to God?

5. Why did Joseph so blatantly favor Benjamin?

Chapter Fourteen

WORST NIGHTMARE

Joseph's brother had feasted to the full because of the amazing generosity of "the man" in Egypt. Things couldn't have been better. They would have an abundance of food to take back to their father, and most importantly, Benjamin was more than safe. Consequently, so were the sons of Reuben.

> And he commanded the steward of his house, saying, "Fill the men's sacks with food, as much as they can carry, and put each man's money in the mouth of his sack. Also put my cup, the silver cup, in the mouth of the sack of the youngest, and his grain money." So he did according to the word that Joseph had spoken. As soon as the morning dawned, the men were sent away, they and their donkeys. When they had gone out of the city, and were not yet far off, Joseph said to his steward, "Get up, follow the men; and when you overtake them, say to them, 'Why have you repaid evil for good? Is not this the one from which my lord drinks, and with which he indeed practices divination? You have done evil in so doing.'"

So he overtook them, and he spoke to them these same words. And they said to him, "Why does my lord say these words? Far be it from us that your servants should do such a thing. Look, we brought back to you from the land of Canaan the money which we found in the mouth of our sacks. How then could we steal silver or gold from your lord's house? With whomever of your servants it is found, let him die, and we also will be my lord's slaves."

And he said, "Now also let it be according to your words; he with whom it is found shall be my slave, and you shall be blameless." Then each man speedily let down his sack to the ground, and each opened his sack. (Genesis 44:1–11)

They "speedily" opened their sacks. They did it quickly because they knew that they were innocent. How could they be so evil in the face of such kindness? This would be resolved in a moment of time.

Sinners are quick to want to be examined by the Commandments, to get this issue of their innocence resolved.

So he searched. He began with the oldest and left off with the youngest; and the cup was found in Benjamin's sack. Then they tore their clothes, and each man loaded his donkey and returned to the city. (verses 12,13)

The cup was found with Benjamin! This couldn't be happening! It was their worst nightmare.

And so it is, when sinners are asked if they are morally good, they speedily boast of their own goodness. Of course they are good; there is no question. They are quick to want to be examined by the Commandments, to get this issue of their innocence resolved. They don't understand the spiritual nature of the Law—that it equates lust with adultery and hatred with murder. As they begin to be searched by the Law, it dawns on them that they have terribly sinned against God, even using His holy name as an expression of disgust. They have returned evil for good. Through the Commandment, sin becomes exceedingly sinful (see Romans 7:13).

> So Judah and his brothers came to Joseph's house, and he was still there; and they fell before him on the ground. And Joseph said to them, "What deed is this you have done? Did you not know that such a man as I can certainly practice divination?"
>
> Then Judah said, "What shall we say to my lord? What shall we speak? Or how shall we clear ourselves? God has found out the iniquity of your servants; here we are, my lord's slaves, both we and he also with whom the cup was found." (verses 14–16)

Notice that all ten brothers returned to Joseph's house. Why did they do that? Do you remember that, though the brothers said the guilty one would die and the rest would become slaves, the steward had responded that "with whom it is found shall be my slave, and you shall be blameless." Benjamin was the guilty one. He was to be a slave, but they were blameless. They were free to return to their father. Yet they didn't. Any one of them could have returned home without blame, but each man returned to the city. They couldn't face their father without Benjamin!

This time they "fell" before Joseph (verse 14). This wasn't because He was Lord of Egypt and controlled the food. This was a prostration of utter humiliation, a begging for mercy because of personal guilt. It was deeper than meets the eye. It wasn't only a guilt because Benjamin was found with the cup, but because they perceived that the hand of God was exposing the terrible evil they had once committed. The iniquity of their past had caught up to them. This was confirmed by what Judah said to Joseph. He didn't talk about the guilt of Benjamin in stealing the cup, but rather confessed (on behalf of his brothers) that "God has found out the iniquity of your servants" (verse 16).

As they offered themselves to be slaves, listen to what Joseph then said to his brothers:

> But he said, "Far be it from me that I should do so; the man in whose hand the cup was found, he shall be my slave. And as for you, go up in peace to your father." (verse 17)

Joseph again gave Judah and his brothers the option to freely go. All they needed to do was leave Benjamin in Egypt and the problem would be solved. All would be well. He even probed the wound by saying "go up in peace to your father." Go back and tell him that he has now lost Benjamin.

One could wonder if this continual testing by Joseph was overkill. But before he brought his brothers into the blessings he had in mind, there needed be a godly sorrow for their crime. And those who come to the Savior must have godly sorrow for their sin, or their repentance won't be "to life" (see Acts 11:18). It will be superficial. The Scriptures say of their uncle, Esau:

> For you know that afterward, when he wanted to inherit the blessing, he was rejected, for he found no place for repentance, though he sought it diligently with tears. (Hebrews 12:17)

Esau had diligence and even tears, but he lacked the godly sorrow which leads to repentance.

> Then Judah came near to him and said: "O my lord, please let your servant speak a word in my lord's hearing, and do not let your anger burn against your servant; for you are even like Pharaoh. My lord asked his servants, saying, 'Have you a father or a brother?' And we said to my lord,

'We have a father, an old man, and a child of his old age, who is young; his brother is dead, and he alone is left of his mother's children, and his father loves him.'" (Genesis 44:18–20)

God only knows what Judah was thinking as he said, "His brother is dead." No doubt the alarm of conscience sounded as he mentioned Joseph. Perhaps Judah saw his brother as being as good as dead. He was nailed to the cross of slavery; he would never return. But Joseph wasn't dead. He stood before Judah alive and well because of the hand of God. We are told, "Then Judah came near to him..."

It is our knowledge of sin that brings us in humility to God. The Scriptures promise:

> Draw near to God and He will draw near to you. Cleanse your hands, you sinners; and purify your hearts, you double-minded. Lament and mourn and weep! Let your laughter be turned to mourning and your joy to gloom. Humble yourselves in the sight of the Lord, and He will lift you up. (James 4:8–10)

> "Come now, and let us reason together,"
> Says the LORD,
> "Though your sins are like scarlet,
> They shall be as white as snow;
> Though they are red like crimson,
> They shall be as wool." (Isaiah 1:18)

Judah continued pleading his case before Joseph:

> "Then you said to your servants, 'Bring him down to me, that I may set my eyes on him.' And we said to my lord, 'The lad cannot leave his father, for if he should leave his father, his father would die.' But you said to your servants, 'Unless your youngest brother comes down with you, you shall see my face no more.'

"So it was, when we went up to your servant my father, that we told him the words of my lord. And our father said, 'Go back and buy us a little food.' But we said, 'We cannot go down; if our youngest brother is with us, then we will go down; for we may not see the man's face unless our youngest brother is with us.' Then your servant my father said to us, 'You know that my wife bore me two sons; and the one went out from me, and I said, "Surely he is torn to pieces"; and I have not seen him since. But if you take this one also from me, and calamity befalls him, you shall bring down my gray hair with sorrow to the grave.'

Here is the deep work of repentance in the guilty sinner. Godly sorrow produces repentance.

"Now therefore, when I come to your servant my father, and the lad is not with us, since his life is bound up in the lad's life, it will happen, when he sees that the lad is not with us, that he will die. So your servants will bring down the gray hair of your servant our father with sorrow to the grave." (Genesis 44:21–31)

Joseph was looking for contrition. Would his brothers be tempted to repeat their sin against their father? They had grieved him beyond words with the lie that Joseph was dead; could they grieve him again? The answer was that it was unthinkable to them. Judah said,

"For your servant became surety for the lad to my father, saying, 'If I do not bring him back to you, then I shall bear the blame before my father forever.' Now therefore, please let your servant remain instead of the lad as a slave to my lord, and let the lad go up with his brothers. For how shall I go up to my father if the lad is not with me, lest perhaps I see the evil that would come upon my father?" (verses 32–34)

Here is the deep work of repentance in the guilty sinner. Godly sorrow produces repentance. The penitent prodigal owns his sins; he has done evil and sinned against Heaven. He doesn't blame God, as did Adam, nor does he blame others. The Law stops his mouth and leaves him guilty before God.

Questions

1. What did finding the cup with Benjamin do to his brothers?
2. Explain the guilt they felt as they lay before Joseph.
3. Explain the meaning of Isaiah 1:18 and how it is fulfilled in Christ.
4. Why must there be godly sorrow in those who approach the cross?
5. Who does the genuine convert blame for his sins?

Chapter Fifteen

LIKE A GUSHING STREAM

Here now is the overwhelming power of love. It can't remain silent. Joseph's secret couldn't be contained any longer. Like a gushing stream, Joseph spills the good news all over his brothers.

> Then Joseph could not restrain himself before all those who stood by him, and he cried out, "Make everyone go out from me!" So no one stood with him while Joseph made himself known to his brothers. And he wept aloud, and the Egyptians and the house of Pharaoh heard it. (Genesis 45:1,2)

Absolute confusion must have fallen on Joseph's brothers. One moment this was a confident and powerful political potentate, who spoke roughly to them and held their very lives within his hands. And the next moment he was having a meltdown—sobbing like a small child.

> Then Joseph said to his brothers, "I am Joseph; does my father still live?" But his brothers could not answer him,

129

for they were dismayed in his presence. And Joseph said to his brothers, "Please come near to me." So they came near. Then he said: "I am Joseph your brother, whom you sold into Egypt. But now, do not therefore be grieved or angry with yourselves because you sold me here; for God sent me before you to preserve life." (verses 3–5)

The band of brothers had good reason to be dismayed in his presence. If this was Joseph, they were dead men. They were guilty of selling him into slavery and he would understandably be bitter and angry.

The band of brothers had good reason to be dismayed in his presence. If this was Joseph, they were dead men.

The Law makes us tremble in our sins. Its wrath makes us both confused and dismayed, with no hope of escape. But in a moment of time the only Potentate—the God who is dark and distant, who thunders out His terrifying wrath upon guilty sinners—is holding out nail-pierced hands in divine love. The glorious gospel of Jesus Christ draws us near and says, "Fear not. Do not be dismayed. Don't be grieved or angry with yourselves. I was betrayed, sold, and then crucified, but God sent Me to preserve life."

"For these two years the famine has been in the land, and there are still five years in which there will be neither plowing nor harvesting. And God sent me before you to preserve a posterity for you in the earth, and to save your lives by a great deliverance. So now it was not you who sent me here, but God; and He has made me a father to Pharaoh, and lord of all his house, and a ruler throughout all the land of Egypt." (verses 6–8)

For God so loved the world that He sent His only begotten Son to preserve us by the greatest of deliverances. The cross was the means by which God saved us from the power of death. This wonderful narrative of God using Joseph to deliver his family from the consequences of a deadly famine is but a shadow of God using Jesus to deliver those He loves from the power of sin and death. William E. Brown said,

> The temporal deliverance so dominant in the Old Testament falls into the background in the New. However, the historical accounts in the Old Testament serve as proof that God is the great deliverer. For example, after recounting examples of God's deliverance, Peter concludes that "the Lord knows how to rescue godly men from trials and to hold the unrighteous for the day of judgment" (2 Peter 2:9)...By God's power, believers are delivered from "this present evil age" (Gal. 1:4) and the power of Satan's reign (Col. 1:13).
>
> The evil impulses that grip the human heart cause Paul's cry for deliverance: "What a wretched man I am! Who will rescue me from this body of death?" (Rom. 7:24). The answer to Paul's cry is "Jesus Christ our Lord" (v. 25). All pleas for deliverance are answered by the person and work of Jesus Christ. He was delivered up for us (Rom. 4:25) that he might deliver us from all that threatens us in this life and in the life to come.
>
> The ultimate deliverance for humankind is from the coming wrath of God on the final day of judgment. Here again, the people of God have hope in "The Deliverer" (Rom. 11:26) who will intervene and save them from the terrible fate reserved for the ungodly: "Jesus, who rescues us from the coming wrath" (1 Thess. 1:10).[17]

After Joseph told his incredulous brothers who he was, he gave credibility to his identity claim by saying that they had sold him into Egypt. He added, "Do not therefore be grieved or angry with yourselves." He forgave them because he loved them.

When Jesus revealed Himself to His disciples after His resurrection, He comforted them and assured them that what had happened to Him was in God's plan. God was in Christ, reconciling the world to Himself:

> Then He said to them, "O foolish ones, and slow of heart to believe in all that the prophets have spoken! Ought not the Christ to have suffered these things and to enter into His glory?" And beginning at Moses and all the Prophets, He expounded to them in all the Scriptures the things concerning Himself. (Luke 24:25–27)

When we come to the Savior we are given the same comfort. There is no longer any condemnation for our sins from the Father, whose good pleasure it is to give us the Kingdom. Ought not the Christ to have suffered? Love demanded it. Our transgressions are now blotted out, washed away, forgiven, and removed as far as the east is from the west, because love covers a multitude of sins.

> "Hurry and go up to my father, and say to him, 'Thus says your son Joseph: "God has made me lord of all Egypt; come down to me, do not tarry. You shall dwell in the land of Goshen, and you shall be near to me, you and your children, your children's children, your flocks and your herds, and all that you have. There I will provide for you, lest you and your household, and all that you have, come to poverty; for there are still five years of famine."'
>
> "And behold, your eyes and the eyes of my brother Benjamin see that it is my mouth that speaks to you. So you shall tell my father of all my glory in Egypt, and of all that you have seen; and you shall hurry and bring my father down here." (Genesis 45:9–13)

Twice, Joseph told his brothers to hurry to tell their father and his children the good news. The famine would not swallow them. God had made Joseph lord of Egypt and he would provide for them according to the riches of his glory.

There is an urgency to reach this dying world. Hurry! Every day 150,000 human beings are swallowed by death. About ten people died as you read that statistic. Many are dying in their sins and will be damned forever. How can we not hurry to preach the good news that death has been destroyed—that Jesus rose from its grasp and has been exalted to the right hand of the Father? God has made Him both Lord and Christ, and He promises to supply all of our needs according to His riches in glory by Christ Jesus.

> *Every day 150,000 human beings are swallowed by death. About ten people died as you read that statistic.*

> Then he fell on his brother Benjamin's neck and wept, and Benjamin wept on his neck. Moreover he kissed all his brothers and wept over them, and after that his brothers talked with him.
>
> Now the report of it was heard in Pharaoh's house, saying, "Joseph's brothers have come." So it pleased Pharaoh and his servants well. And Pharaoh said to Joseph, "Say to your brothers, 'Do this: Load your animals and depart; go to the land of Canaan. Bring your father and your households and come to me; I will give you the best of the land of Egypt, and you will eat the fat of the land. Now you are commanded—do this: Take carts out of the land of Egypt for your little ones and your wives; bring your father and come. Also do not be concerned about your goods, for the best of all the land of Egypt is yours.'" (verses 14–20)

The best of all the earth will be ours. We are going to inherit this amazing planet. Skeptics in their ignorance think that our hope for eternity is a nebulous and boring existence in a ghostly Heaven—not knowing that Heaven is coming to this earth and God's will will be done on this old earth as it is in Heaven. We are awaiting a new heavens and a new earth in which righteousness dwells. No more sin—murder, hatred, greed, jealousy, and corruption. And also no more disease, suffering, decay, and death. This fallen earth will be restored to Eden. No eye has ever seen nor ear ever heard of the incredible things that God has prepared for those who love Him. The song of birds, the glory of a sunrise, the blueness of the sky, the white sands of a tropical shore, the taste of our most luscious food, the joy of the marital bed, and a million other pleasures of this passing life are endlessly tedious, painfully dull, and unbearably boring compared to what God has eternally in store for those who love Him.

Do you love Him? Have you seen your sins? Are you contrite before the Holy One of Israel? And have you seen His love in the cross? Have you found everlasting life in Jesus? Then why are you gazing up into the heavens? Run with urgency to this dying world and shout from the housetops the glad tidings of the gospel.

> Then the sons of Israel did so; and Joseph gave them carts, according to the command of Pharaoh, and he gave them provisions for the journey. He gave to all of them, to each man, changes of garments; but to Benjamin he gave three hundred pieces of silver and five changes of garments. And he sent to his father these things: ten donkeys loaded with the good things of Egypt, and ten female donkeys loaded with grain, bread, and food for his father for the journey. So he sent his brothers away, and they departed; and he said to them, "See that you do not become troubled along the way." (verses 21–24)

Let not your heart be troubled along the way. We have the provision of God as we tread the path to the promised land of the Kingdom. Trials will come, but we are more than conquerors through Him who loved us. By faith in God, we rise above them.

> Then they went up out of Egypt, and came to the land of Canaan to Jacob their father. And they told him, saying, "Joseph is still alive, and he is governor over all the land of Egypt." And Jacob's heart stood still, because he did not believe them. But when they told him all the words which Joseph had said to them, and when he saw the carts which Joseph had sent to carry him, the spirit of Jacob their father revived. (verses 25–27)

Christ has risen from the dead. He is still alive, seated at the right hand of the Father, and is Lord over all. Our spirit is eternally revived.

> "The kingdoms of this world have become the kingdoms of our Lord and of His Christ, and He shall reign forever and ever!" (Revelation 11:15)

Questions

1. What drove Joseph to reveal himself to his brothers?
2. What should drive us to reach out to the unsaved?
3. Why is there an urgency to do so?
4. What is going to happen to this earth?
5. Is your hope in Jesus?

Chapter Sixteen

BEFORE I DIE

Jacob had heard the unbelievable, but now he believed. His dead son—whose shed blood he believed that he had seen—was alive!

> Then Israel said, "It is enough. Joseph my son is still alive. I will go and see him before I die." (Genesis 45:28)

It is enough. Coming to the risen Savior is all that matters in this life. Jesus came back from the dead. Death could not hold Him. Everything else fades into obscurity in the light of our eternal salvation. Who we married, how many children we had, what we achieved—our legacy, our fame, and our fortune will mean nothing on the Day of Judgment. All that matters will be, "Are we justified in Christ?" Are we wearing a white robe? If we are, we will live; if we are not, we will be damned.

> Riches do not profit in the day of wrath, but righteousness delivers from death. (Proverbs 11:4)

It is this knowledge coupled with the love of God in us that drives us to reach out to the lost. The good news of the gospel should gush from our lips. We want the world to say, "I will go and see Jesus before I die." I will therefore devote these final chapters to the most honorable of goals—following Jesus in seeking to save that which is lost.

The story of Joseph has all the makings of a secular hit movie: the undying love of a father, jealousy, hatred, kidnapping, great character development, Potiphar's lusty wife, her consequential lies, intrigue, prison life, dreams and the supernatural, and a tear-jerker happy ending.

The Bible is mocked by skeptics, because it contains stories that are unbelievable in the truest sense of the word.

It rarely fails to make me weep when I read of how Joseph revealed himself to his brothers. It's one of the narratives that makes the Bible the world's most beloved Book.

Yet the same Bible is mocked by skeptics, because it also contains stories that are unbelievable in the truest sense of the word. One among many is the story of Adam and Eve—particularly the serpent talking with Eve—and is mockingly referred to in some cynic circles as "the talking snake." This, and a number of other Bible stories, can be a hindrance for some when it comes to believing the gospel. How do we reach these people? It is like trying to convince someone to believe that Cinderella really did have a coach that turned into a pumpkin at midnight. To make an important point, I would like to talk for a moment (with a little tongue-in-cheek) about that talking snake.

The Bible does speak of a literal serpent that walked upright and spoke audibly to Eve:

But I fear, lest somehow, as the serpent deceived Eve by his craftiness, so your minds may be corrupted from the simplicity that is in Christ. (2 Corinthians 11:3)

If you stop reading these words, and think about what you are reading, you will be talking to yourself inside your head. Scientists call this "inner speech":

Most of us will be familiar with the experience of silently talking to ourselves in our head. Perhaps you're at the supermarket and realise that you've forgotten to pick up something you needed. "Milk!" you might say to yourself. Or maybe you've got an important meeting with your boss later in the day, and you're simulating—silently in your head—how you think the conversation might go, possibly hearing both your own voice and your boss's voice responding.

This is the phenomenon that psychologists call "inner speech", and they've been trying to study it pretty much since the dawn of psychology as a scientific discipline.[18]

This inner speech is much faster than conventional speech:

One researcher…clocks inner speech at an average pace of 4,000 words per minute—10 times faster than verbal speech. And it's often more condensed—we don't have to use full sentences to talk to ourselves, because we know what we mean.[19]

Do you think that snakes think? They must have thoughts, in order to seek out what they will eat and drink, where they will go, and what predators they should avoid. While these thoughts could be written off as unthought instinct, the snake has a brain and it's not too much of a stretch to think that brains are for thinking. Which perhaps brings us to the conclusion that snakes do cogitate as we do, though it's not vocalized.

The argument, therefore, should be about snakes not having vocal cords. Contemporary snakes don't have the ability to express their thoughts vocally, while this serpent in the Bible did.

It's also not too much of a stretch to say that dogs can "speak." They normally communicate with each other through a language we don't understand, although they sometimes do this in a language we do understand. I know when a stranger comes through the gate of our home because my dog informs me that a stranger is on our property and there is potential danger. At that moment we share the same language:

> Animal signalling systems are not (as far as we can tell) as complex as human language, nor do they fit the linguist's definition of a language—the existence of grammar, syntax, and sound units. "Words in languages are finite, but sentences are not. It is this creative aspect of human language that sets it apart from animal languages, which are essentially responses to stimuli," write Victoria Fromkin and Robert Rodman, expressing the semantic view.
>
> But dogs do have many ways of telling us things. When a puppy wags its tail or barks or runs around in circles as we arrive home from work, we get the gist. *I'm hungry. Let's go for a walk! Get off of my property.* And mounting evidence shows that dogs understand human language better than previously assumed (except by dog lovers). They're about as smart as a 2- or 3-year-old child, the age at which most kids begin to initiate conversations and speak in simple sentences.[20]

OTHER "SPEAKING" ANIMALS

The rooster announces that morning is near, the cat communicates when he's hungry, frogs croak at night, sheep bleat so that they can locate each other, and scientists tell us that porpoises have a complex language in which they talk to each other, as do whales.

And of course primates have the ability to communicate. According to *Smithsonian Magazine*, "'Talking' apes are not just the stuff of science fiction; scientists have taught many apes to use some semblance of language."[21]

> Most primates live in groups in which members know each other individually and maintain multifaceted social relations, factors which are thought to favour the evolution of advanced communication skills (McComb & Semple 2005). However, other animals with complex social behaviour, such as dolphins, also show sophisticated communication skills, suggesting that complex communication is not limited to primates (Janik 2009).[22]

Yet, there's an irony in the atheist's mockery of the talking snake. His worldview dictates that it is absurd for evolution to have given a reptile vocal cords so that it could speak. But he believes that he is an animal that evolved vocal cords, so he can speak.

Anyone who believes in Darwinian evolution believes that human beings are talking primates, as *Smithsonian Magazine* declares:

> I'm a primate. You're a primate. Everyone reading this blog is a primate. That's not news. We hear it all he time: Humans are primates.[23]

OUR BIG PROBLEM

When we try to explain talking snakes to a skeptic, our big problem is that it takes us down a time-consuming rabbit trail. Whether or not snakes could manifest their thoughts shouldn't be the issue. This is because our agenda isn't to get anyone to concede that a snake could talk, that walls could fall down with a shout, that the sun could stand still, that a large fish could swallow a man and he lives, that Lot's wife turned into a pillar of salt, or that Samson killed a thousand Philistines with a donkey's jawbone. We could go through each of these hard-to-swallow incidents (as we did with the talking snake) and perhaps get some intellectual concessions from a reasonable skeptic.

But there are still huge hurdles for him to wrap his skeptical mind around: Jesus walking on water, speaking to a storm and having it obey Him, talking to dead people and having them come back to life, etc.

We should talk of the Law and convince a sinner that he is in danger and desperately needs the Savior.

So our agenda, rather, is to convince the sinner to say, "I will go and see Jesus before I die." As we have seen earlier, there is an easier way to do this, and it's simply to do what Jesus did with those we call unbelievers.

Let's take for example the unseen force of electricity. Invisible though it is, because of it we can communicate through our phones at the speed of light with anyone on the planet. If there is no electricity in your phone's battery, you're not going to speak with anyone. Electricity opens the door to a miraculous experience we so take for granted that we do a double take when the word "miraculous" is used to describe it. But two hundred years ago, that description would be thoroughly appropriate, even if the supernatural wasn't involved.

We experience all sorts of amazing things because of invisible electricity—movies, television, WiFi, lighting, heating, cooling, digital clocks, elevators, motor vehicles, iPads, iPods, USB drives, flashlights, etc. All are made possible by an invisible force that no one has ever seen: electricity.

There are a couple reasons you cannot directly see electricity. The first reason is because electricity is a phenomenon, not a physical object. We observe certain phenomena in nature through their interaction with physical objects (which we can see). Take the phenomenon of gravity, for example. You cannot technically "see" gravity, though you can observe objects that fall to the ground or cannonballs/projectiles that follow a trajectory suggestive of force "pulling" them to the earth. The same is true of electricity. We can observe electricity's influence in nature in the same way as gravity, though there's one really important difference and the main reason you can't see it:

The fundamental components on which electricity is observed are really really small, move really really fast and there's a lot of them. The reason you can't see electricity is the same reason you can't see an individual electron (too small) or a bullet fired from a gun (too fast) or accurately guess how many jelly beans are in large jar (too many).[24]

If I wanted to convince a skeptic that electricity is a reality, I could take the long route and center on how a phone or iPad or WiFi works. Or I could save myself a lot of time and effort by having him hold onto a live low-voltage electrical wire to personally experience its power.

The gospel is the live wire. As "the power of God to salvation for everyone who believes" (Romans 1:16), the gospel convinces the most doubting of Thomases to fall at the feet of Jesus and cry, "My Lord and my God" and go to see Jesus before he dies.

Discussing talking snakes, etc., stays in the carnal and contentious human intellect, and that's a battle we need not enter (interesting though it may be). Instead, we should talk of the Law and convince a sinner that he is in danger and desperately needs the Savior. That's the battle in which we must continually contend.

PLEASURE FORTIFICATION

It's always important to remember that the average atheist isn't seeking truth. He is wanting to fortify his own position, so that he can continue to indulge in the pleasures of sin without a nagging sense of guilt.

In August 2018, the leader of an atheist group in Southern California asked if we could have lunch together. I was happy to spend time with Bruce, but wondered if he had an ulterior motive.

Just before he arrived at our ministry, I found out what that was. He wanted to do a "five-minute" interview with me after we had eaten.

A few years ago he filmed a sword fight between us and the clip had received hundreds of thousands of views. It seemed that he was wanting to get that sort of attention again.

After lunch, he set up his phone in front of me for filming and then, while he was off-camera, he began the first of what he said would be thirteen questions.

As we went through each one, I noticed that if I didn't give the answer he wanted, he would talk over me, cut me off, and then go to the next question. I also noticed that his questions were manipulative. They were phrased like, "Ray, why is it that all intelligent scientists are atheists?" If I said that it wasn't true, and that all scientists weren't atheists, he would talk over my answer and quickly move on to the next question. As I battled to answer one after the other I began to regret doing the interview.

Finally, he got to question thirteen, where he preempted it by saying that it was his trump card, and he wanted me to elaborate on it. The question was, "Is there anything that would change your mind about the existence of God?" This was designed to paint me as a closed-minded, anti-science bigot. I said, "Is there anything that would change your mind about the existence of your wife?" Then I explained to him that as a Christian I have a relationship with God, and it has nothing to do with a "belief" that God exists. I didn't have "faith" that a builder built the building in which we were sitting. I told him that I knew there was a builder because buildings don't build themselves.

When we as Christians speak of faith, we are not talking about the existence of God. Creation/nature is evidence of that. Rather, we are talking about an implicit trust in the integrity of God to keep His Word. The Scriptures say that it is impossible for God to lie, and that means we can rely on everything He says as absolute truth.

> *When we as Christians speak of faith, we are not talking about the existence of God.*

He didn't like that answer either, and after about ten minutes of talking over me he decided to end the interview, which by now had taken twenty long and frustrating minutes.

Bruce picked up his phone, turned it over, and then let out a loud expletive. He had forgotten to turn the camera on. He then packed up his equipment, sarcastically mumbling something about God causing him to forget to turn it on.

As usual with staunch atheists, he hadn't been seeking truth. The whole exercise was just another effort to justify his belief in the insanity of atheism—the scientific impossibility that nothing created everything.

Questions

1. Do you have inner speech? How would you describe it?
2. Do you think that animals think? Why?

3. If you have a dog, in what ways does he or she speak to you?

4. What are we to convince the secular world about?

5. Relate the analogy of using electricity to convincing someone of the power of the gospel.

Chapter Seventeen

THE PIGS

We have to choose our words when we speak to the world. Those who follow the Good Shepherd are an abomination to some, who hate our faithful Creator without cause and hate those who belong to Him. But, if our speech is seasoned with grace, we can make our way through this evil world without compromising our faith. Discretion is a forgotten art among many today, but it wasn't missing with Joseph.

He primed his brothers, and his father's household, by saying, "I will go up and tell Pharaoh, and say to him, 'My brothers and those of my father's house, who were in the land of Canaan, have come to me. And the men are shepherds, for their occupation has been to feed livestock; and they have brought their flocks, their herds, and all that they have'" (Genesis 46:31,32). He said that he wouldn't hide the fact that they were shepherds, but he would assure Pharaoh that they would be self-sufficient. Then Joseph told them what to say when they faced him:

"So it shall be, when Pharaoh calls you and says, 'What is your occupation?' that you shall say, 'Your servants' occupation has been with livestock from our youth even till now, both we and also our fathers,' that you may dwell in the land of Goshen; for every shepherd is an abomination to the Egyptians." (Genesis 46:33,34)

Luke 15 is one of my many favorite Bible passages. This is because the entire chapter stays with one theme:

Then all the tax collectors and the sinners drew near to Him to hear Him. And the Pharisees and scribes complained, saying, "This Man receives sinners and eats with them." (Luke 15:1,2)

Sinners were lost and He came to find them; they were under His wrath, and He came to forgive them.

As the Egyptians despised every shepherd, so the Pharisees despised Jesus and the sinners He received. And that's the theme in this passage. Jesus received sinners. He spoke with them, embraced them, taught, listened to, and ate and drank with them. He was the friend of sinners. They were lost and He came to find them; they were under His wrath, and He came to forgive them. That's why He received them. So to bring home the point to the blind Pharisees and scribes, Jesus spoke about a shepherd, the first of three parables:

"What man of you, having a hundred sheep, if he loses one of them, does not leave the ninety-nine in the wilderness, and go after the one which is lost until he finds it? And when he has found it, he lays it on his shoulders, rejoicing. And when he comes home, he calls together his friends and neighbors, saying to them, 'Rejoice with me, for I have found my sheep which was lost!' I say to you that likewise there will be more joy in heaven over one sinner who repents than over ninety-nine just persons who need no repentance." (verses 4–7)

Perhaps Joseph had had this experience as a young shepherd. One sheep strayed, and he left his entire flock and searched until he found it. This thought shows us that one sheep is greatly valued by a good shepherd. If one dumb sheep went missing from a flock of one hundred, it wouldn't even be noticeable to many. But this shepherd of whom Jesus spoke both knew it was missing and searched until he found it.

If that wasn't Joseph's experience as a young shepherd, it was certainly his experience as a lost sheep. The Good Shepherd found him and stayed with him through life's trials.

The found sheep of whom Jesus spoke is seen to be further valued by the shepherd's rejoicing after he found it. He didn't put a rope around its neck and drag it back to the flock. He instead lifted it onto his shoulders. He raised it to a place of safety, of protection from predators. If a wolf were to attack it, it would have to attack the shepherd first.

This is wonderfully consoling for Christians. It's a picture of how God loves and cares for us. But it also shows us that the unsaved are greatly valued by Him. They are to be loved and sought out. That is where we should be putting our energies. Evangelism should be our number one priority. Is it yours and mine? Look again at these wonderful words:

"I say to you that likewise there will be more joy in heaven over one sinner who repents than over ninety-nine just persons who need no repentance." (verse 7)

When a sinner repents, it brings joy to Heaven. What Jesus said was very clear. But to further make the point of God's will for the lost being our priority, He said the same thing again from a different perspective. He goes from sheep to coins:

> "Or what woman, having ten silver coins, if she loses one coin, does not light a lamp, sweep the house, and search carefully until she finds it? And when she has found it, she calls her friends and neighbors together, saying, 'Rejoice with me, for I have found the piece which I lost!' Likewise, I say to you, there is joy in the presence of the angels of God over one sinner who repents." (verses 8–10)

This is like with Pharaoh's disturbing dreams, where God used cows to illustrate a point and then He emphasized it by using grain to say the same thing. Here Jesus uses the example of sheep, and then emphasized it with coins. When one coin was lost, this woman turned on the light and searched diligently until she found it. She did this because she valued the coin.

Jesus has used a lost sheep and then a lost coin to make the point that we should be passionately reaching out to a lost world. But the church as a whole doesn't do that. After decades of trying to get the body of Christ to reach out to the lost, I have to wonder if they have ever read these verses. In most churches everything is prioritized except for evangelism. It is the last caboose on the train.

And so Jesus moved from animals and coins to human beings to emphasize the same point, but with wonderful detail:

> Then He said: "A certain man had two sons. And the younger of them said to his father, 'Father, give me the portion of goods that falls to me.' So he divided to them his livelihood. And not many days after, the younger son gathered all together, journeyed to a far country, and there wasted his possessions with prodigal living." (verses 11–13)

The son's hormones had kicked in and he was looking for a Potiphar's wife—a loose woman who would lie with him in exchange for money. We know this because later in the story the prodigal's brother spills the beans. Perhaps the prodigal told him before he left how he was burning and needed his flame put out. He, like Moses, enjoyed the pleasures of sin for a season (see Hebrews 11:25). Things were humming for the prodigal, until a time of trial appeared:

> But when he had spent all, there arose a severe famine in that land, and he began to be in want. Then he went and joined himself to a citizen of that country, and he sent him into his fields to feed swine. And he would gladly have filled his stomach with the pods that the swine ate, and no one gave him anything.
>
> "But when he came to himself, he said, 'How many of my father's hired servants have bread enough and to spare, and I perish with hunger! I will arise and go to my father, and will say to him, "Father, I have sinned against heaven and before you, and I am no longer worthy to be called your son. Make me like one of your hired servants."' And he arose and came to his father." (verses 14–20)

Famine brought Jacob to his senses so that he let go of Benjamin before they all starved to death, and famine did the same with the prodigal. It made him think of his father and of his own sinful heart. It was the realization that his desires were for filthy pig food that brought him to his senses. And it is when you and I realize that our desires are for the filth of sin that we come to our senses. It is the Law that shows our moral famine—that sin is exceedingly sinful. It stirs the conscience, revealing to us that we are all as an unclean thing and all of our righteousnesses are as filthy rags—as the Holy Spirit convicts us of sin, of righteousness, and of judgment to come.

Then as the son turns to the father in repentance, here comes the glorious wonder of the cross:

"But when he was still a great way off, his father saw him and had compassion, and ran and fell on his neck and kissed him." (verse 20)

When we were still a great way off, the Father saw us and ran to the cross in Christ. It was His good pleasure to give us the Kingdom. It was in that terrible suffering that He showed His great compassion. It was in the blood of the cross that He fell on our neck and kissed us:

But God demonstrates His own love toward us, in that while we were still sinners, Christ died for us. (Romans 5:8)

The arms of the Father were stretched out in Christ on the cross. He was in Christ reconciling the world to Himself.

"And the son said to him, 'Father, I have sinned against heaven and in your sight, and am no longer worthy to be called your son.'

"But the father said to his servants, 'Bring out the best robe and put it on him, and put a ring on his hand and sandals on his feet. And bring the fatted calf here and kill it, and let us eat and be merry; for this my son was dead and is alive again; he was lost and is found.' And they began to be merry." (Luke 15:20–24)

Joseph was taken from prison, washed, and dressed to appear before Pharaoh, and we are taken from the prison of sin and death and clothed in the perfect righteousness of Christ. We are made pure in heart so that we can see God. And all Heaven rejoices.

"Now his older son was in the field. And as he came and drew near to the house, he heard music and dancing. So he called one of the servants and asked what these things meant. And he said to him, 'Your brother has come, and because he has received him safe and sound, your father has killed the fatted calf.'

"But he was angry and would not go in. Therefore his father came out and pleaded with him. So he answered and said to his father, 'Lo, these many years I have been serving you; I never transgressed your commandment at any time; and yet you never gave me a young goat, that I might make merry with my friends. But as soon as this son of yours came, who has devoured your livelihood with harlots, you killed the fatted calf for him.'

"And he said to him, 'Son, you are always with me, and all that I have is yours. It was right that we should make merry and be glad, for your brother was dead and is alive again, and was lost and is found.'" (verses 25–32)

Which of the two brothers are you and I today? Do we have the cold attitude of the unloving brother, or the loving heart of the prodigal's father? We will show which one we are by our actions toward those who are lost... whether or not we receive sinners.

Questions

1. What three illustrations did Jesus use to show us Heaven's priority?
2. Why did He repeat the same thing?
3. What has been your experience with the church's concern for the unsaved?
4. What brought you to the Savior?
5. What are you actively doing to seek and save the lost?

Chapter Eighteen

THE "LIE" DETECTOR

Joseph is not only a type of Christ, but also a type of the Christian. We have been favored by God—chosen by the Father, given a robe of righteousness, mocked and hated by the world, delivered from the pit of death, become a slave to the world, having escaped the corruption that is in the world through lust, accused by the god of this world, delivered by the hand of God from the prison of sin, and exalted to be seated with Christ at the right hand of God, ruling and reigning with Him forever.

Although there is no mention of it in Scripture, I can't help but wonder if Jacob struggled with bitterness against his own sons once he discovered how they treated Joseph. What they had done was unforgivable. They lied to their own father about his son's death, and in so doing put Jacob into a prison of grief (and perhaps guilt) for thirteen long years. Perhaps Jacob also had the added guilt in thinking he may have caused his sons' jealousy by favoring Joseph. Whatever the case, Jacob had the evident example of forgiveness in

Joseph. Joseph had been terribly wronged and yet his great love covered a multitude of sins.

We may have been horribly wronged by others. But we look to our example—to Him who was reviled, rejected, and nailed to a cross, and yet uttered, "Father, forgive them, for they do not know what they do" (Luke 23:34). If Jesus could forgive from the cross, we must do the same through the cross.

Joseph, with all his trials and tribulations, shines as an example of a godly life well-lived.

Joseph is just one colorful character among many in the world's most beloved Book. His amazing story stands out from the others because of his godly character. He didn't miss out on the promised land as did Moses, or stray with foreign women as did Solomon and Samson. The list goes on—from Adam, to King Saul, to David and Bathsheba, we find sinful men and women who fell from a place of grace.

But Joseph, with all his trials and tribulations, shines as an example of a godly life well-lived. These things were written for our instruction.

SOBER INSTRUCTION

An American couple, Jay Austin and Lauren Geoghegan, decided to spend their life savings to bike and blog their way around the world. In August 2018, the two twenty-nine-year-olds were run over and killed in an ISIS-claimed attack in Tajikistan:

> "You read the papers and you're led to believe that the world is a big, scary place," Mr. Austin wrote. "People, the narrative goes, are not to be trusted. People are bad. People are evil . . .

"I don't buy it. Evil is a make-believe concept we've invented to deal with the complexities of fellow humans holding values and beliefs and perspectives different than our own...By and large, humans are kind. Self-interested sometimes, myopic sometimes, but kind. Generous and wonderful and kind. No greater revelation has come from our journey than this," he wrote.

In the video released by the Islamic State after the couple's death, men pledging allegiance to the group can be seen sitting on a stone slab, an aquamarine lake partly visible over their left shoulders. It's the kind of panorama that the young couple might have stopped to capture and post on their blog.

But in the clip, when these men point to the scenery around them, they vow to slaughter the "disbelievers" who have overrun their land.[25]

The worldview of the ungodly is that humanity is good, and if people do evil it's because of some mitigating circumstance in their life that pushed them off the rails. The young man's idea that "evil is a make-believe concept" is more than likely his reference to the biblical concept of sin. I can only guess at that, but I have heard the same wording many times from the unsaved who are taking a swipe at the Christian worldview.

The Bible doesn't simply say that human nature is sinful, it says that we are desperately wicked to the core:

The heart is deceitful above all things, and desperately wicked; who can know it? (Jeremiah 17:9)

Receiving this basic instruction from the Word of God will save us a lot of pain. It will mean that we thoroughly read contracts we are about to sign, check the locks on the doors of our homes, look at our surroundings if we have to walk somewhere at night, carefully choose friends we trust, and don't let our teenage daughter go running by herself. Many a young woman has been raped and murdered because naive parents were of the opinion that human nature is good and that the world is a safe place. Thousands of innocent people are murdered each year just in the United States because the world is not a safe place. If the restraint of the law was removed from society and people could kill those who annoyed them on the freeway, at work, or in the home during a domestic dispute, we would see how evil man really is. And this evil isn't something that is caused by extenuating circumstances. Jesus told us where it originates:

> "For out of the heart proceed evil thoughts, murders, adulteries, fornications, thefts, false witness, blasphemies." (Matthew 15:19)

The human heart is a bubbling reservoir of evil. I know that to be true because I know my own wicked heart.

WE ROBBED A BANK

Many years ago we did an episode of our television program, *Way of the Master*, on this subject. Kirk Cameron and I played bank robbers who were arrested, and Kirk was subjected to a lie detector test. It was then that we had an expert explain that the detector isn't actually a lie detector. Rather, it detects guilt. When the conscience does its God-given duty, our heart pumps a little harder and the skin surface changes slightly. It detects that change when we lie.

If we have our conscience primed and tender, we will feel our temperature rise ever so slightly when we sin. It may be a sudden awareness of raised blood pressure, or an increased heart rate, but you will know it when it happens. That's the moment we either enlighten or deceive ourselves. It's the moment we should say, "Potiphar's wife is calling me and I should run," or, "I shouldn't eat this," "I shouldn't take this," or "I shouldn't say this about that person."

The Scriptures warn us to guard our heart with all diligence (see Proverbs 4:23). If we are walking in the fear of the Lord we will be diligent to listen to the voice of conscience, and will say, "How could I do this thing and sin against God?"

In June 2018, I had been preaching open air in Huntington Beach, California. My friend Stuart Scott was on vacation so I had gone alone. I parked my car, preached for an hour, got back into the vehicle and backed out of my parking spot. It was then that I realized I'd forgotten to buy a ticket for the parking lot. I'd parked for an hour and there wasn't a notice of a $50 fine under my windshield wiper.

During the preaching, I had been reasoning with a young man about how his conscience was like a smoke detector, and how foolish we would be to remove its batteries because we didn't like being alarmed by it. I had also spoken to him about how theft has nothing to do with the value of the stolen item.

I had stolen from the Huntington Beach authorities by not paying. So I backed into the spot, went to the parking machine, paid the meager $1.75, and left. The world may scoff at such a triviality, but we don't love the world, and neither do we live to please its patrons.

On another occasion Scotty and I had been open-air preaching for a couple of hours. We returned to our car in the parking garage and stopped to pay the attendant. To our surprise, he handed our ticket back to us and said that there was no charge. When Scotty said that we thought he'd made a mistake, he said that we hadn't been parked long enough to incur a cost.

Scotty disagreed and asked him to double-check. Sure enough, the attendant was mistaken. As we handed him the payment and a gospel tract we heard him say, "Thank you for being so honorable."

These incidents should be normal conduct for a Christian. Jesus said, "He who is faithful in what is least is faithful also in much; and he who is unjust in what is least is unjust also in much" (Luke 16:10).

Another way to detect sin at the door is to listen to your thoughts. When you're doing something that is questionable, are you trying to justify it? Is your inner voice saying, "It's just a small piece of cake. This is no big deal." Or, "This is just one pen I'm taking from work. I'm a hard worker, so it's not really stealing," etc.

The trials will be endless, keeping us humble, thankful, and on the safety of our knees.

After this do you want to open the Bible or whisper a loving word to your Heavenly Father, or is there a subtle turning of your back toward Him and His Word? If you take the easy path and let sin have its way, you will find yourself to be just like Adam. You will want to hide from God, try to justify yourself, or blame others. That's when you are entering the darkness of self-deception.

Instead, quickly come to the light. Fear God. Think of the cross and what it took for you to be forgiven. Whisper, "Search me, O God, and know my heart; try me, and know my anxieties; and see if there is any wicked way in me, and lead me in the way everlasting" (Psalm 139:23,24).

If we don't come to the light, we can be sure that God, in His faithfulness, will chasten us, because He loves us. The trials will be endless, keeping us humble, thankful, and on the safety of our knees. If that's the case, then I should welcome their wet and webbed feet.

One of my least favorite things to do in life is to visit the dentist. I know that I should go more often, but I tend to wait until I feel the need to go, and some pain does the convincing. This is because I'm not excited about someone stuffing his fingers in my mouth, then causing me terrible pain, and giving me a bill when he's finished.

The sinner will only come to the Savior if he sees his need. We must therefore bring pain to his conscience so that he will desire to come to the cross.

My optometrist (who doesn't cause me any pain) told me that my eyes were in good health, and reminded me to always wear sunglasses. It's a habit that I've had for years and perhaps that was one of the reasons why my eyes were healthy. However, once or twice when I've been driving my car and couldn't find my sunglasses, I realized I was wearing them! I feel foolish when that happens, and it happens because putting my sunglasses on has become second-nature to me. So much so that I often have no recollection of putting them on.

That should be our experience with evangelism. Looking at sinners through the lens of eternity should be second nature to us. We shouldn't even have to consciously think about it; we just do it.

JACOB AND JOSEPH

In John chapter 4, in speaking of Jesus arriving in Samaria, the Scriptures refer to a piece of ground that Jacob gave to his beloved son Joseph:

> So He came to a city of Samaria which is called Sychar, near the plot of ground that Jacob gave to his son Joseph. (John 4:5)

This is in reference to when Jacob was on his deathbed:

Then Israel said to Joseph, "Behold, I am about to die, but God will be with you, and bring you back to [Canaan] the land of your fathers. Moreover, I have given you [the birthright,] one portion [Shechem, one mountain ridge] more than any of your brothers, which I took [reclaiming it] from the hand of the Amorites with my sword and with my bow." (Genesis 48:21,22, AMP)

Jacob gave Joseph "more than any of your brothers." It seems he was still the favored son.

In Christ we have been given undeserved favor by our Heavenly Father. It is His good pleasure to give us the Kingdom. His favor isn't based on our performance but only on His mercy. That means it is steadfast even in the dark hours, and there are plenty of them in this life.

Don't be surprised if trials are lining up to hit you one after the other. Just make sure you don't let them get you down.

Emeal "E.Z." Zwayne said that life is filled with "piles and piles of trials." Try as we may to fortify ourselves against a fallen creation with its never-ending problems, it's like trying to stop leaks in a rainstorm when you have a roof full of holes. Fix one leak and you find ten more. You get rid of the mice in the garage and they nest under the house. The AC is repaired costing an arm and a leg, and then the car breaks down. Pacify Aunt Martha, and Uncle Arthur gets upset. And so life goes, with masses of quacking ducks.

We often hear the phrase, "It's just one thing after another." As we have seen, this is especially true for the Christian. The birds keep coming. The Bible doesn't just say that we enter the Kingdom of God through tribulation, it says we enter the Kingdom of God through "many tribulations" (Acts 14:22).

So don't be surprised if the world hates you, and don't be surprised if trials are lining up to hit you one after the other. Again, just make sure you don't let them get you down. Remember that the only way they will suffocate you is if you lose your faith in God. If that happens you will lose your joy, and the joy of the Lord is your strength.

Be like Joseph. Keep your heart free from sin. Live to interpret the mystery of life for a lost and blind world. Strengthen feeble knees. Lift up hands that hang down, and rejoice that God is working all things together for good because you love Him and are called according to His purpose.

Questions

1. How do you overcome "justified" bitterness, when you are wronged?

2. How would you answer someone who said that there is no such thing as evil?

3. What did Jesus say proceeds from the human heart?

4. Why should we be concerned with small sins?

5. Why shouldn't we be surprised if the world hates us, or when trials seem unending?

NOTES

1. John MacArthur, *The MacArthur Study Bible* (Nashville: Thomas Nelson, 1997).

2. Geoff Thomas, "Nakedness and Gambling on Golgotha," Alfred Place Baptist Church, Oct. 23, 2005.

3. C. H. Spurgeon, "Refusing to Be Comforted," delivered March 18, 1883, at the Metropolitan Tabernacle, Newington.

4. Euan McKirdy and Caroline Kwok, "Woman kills parents, takes her own life over eczema torment," CNN, June 20, 2018.

5. Kathleen Joyce, "New video shows woman trying to resist YouTube stunt that killed boyfriend," Fox News, June 23, 2018 <tinyurl.com/y6es9ola>.

6. John Bingham, "Richard Dawkins: I can't be sure God does not exist," *The Telegraph*, Feb. 24, 2012 <tinyurl.com/ydygj8ms>.

7. Tom Frank, "Lies, coverups mask root of small aircraft carnage," *USA TODAY*, June 18, 2014 <tinyurl.com/y7t6u3xx>.

8. Steve Sternberg, "Medical Errors Are Third Leading Cause of Death in the U.S.," *U.S. News & World Report*, May 3, 2016 <tinyurl.com/kdzn5kc>.

9. Karen Kaplan, "Are elevators really hazardous to your health?" *Los Angeles Times*, December 15, 2011 <tinyurl.com/gqb2l8n>.

10. C. H. Spurgeon, *Morning and Evening: Daily Readings*, Evening, February 20.

11. "Pervert used pen camera to secretly take photos up woman's skirt in McDonald's," *The Sun*, February 13, 2018 <tinyurl.com/yafta7bp>.

12. Danielle Demetriou, "Adultery is good for your marriage—if you don't get caught, says infidelity website boss," *The Telegraph*, April 12, 2014 <tinyurl.com/y7c2feru>.

13. "German pharmacist gets 12 years for diluting cancer drugs," Associated Press, July 6, 2018 <tinyurl.com/ydblosoz>.

14. Pam Belluck, "Prosecutors Say Greed Drove Pharmacist to Dilute Drugs," *New York Times*, August 18, 2001 <tinyurl.com/ycrpuu87>.

15. Gemma Mullin, "No more Walkie Scorchie! London skyscraper which melted cars by reflecting sunlight is fitted with shading," Dailymail.com, October 9, 2014 <tinyurl.com/n6gq388>.

16. Albert Einstein, *The World As I See It* (New York: Philosophical Library, 1949), 13.

17. William E. Brown, "Deliver," *Baker's Evangelical Dictionary of Biblical Theology* <tinyurl.com/ybxhbrvv>.

18. Peter Moseley, "Talking to ourselves: the science of the little voice in your head," *The Guardian*, August 21, 2014 <tinyurl.com/ztc9m7s>.

19. Julie Beck, "The Running Conversation in Your Head," *The Atlantic*, November 23, 2016 <tinyurl.com/hey2d2m>.

20. Megan Erickson, "Do Dogs Speak Human?" BigThink.com, June, 29, 2012 <tinyurl.com/y7dnlwma>.

21. Erin Wayman, "Six Talking Apes," *Smithsonian Magazine*, August 11, 2011 <tinyurl.com/ydfhjsem>.

22. Klaus Zuberbuhler, "Primate Communication," *Nature Education Knowledge* (2012) 3(10):83 <tinyurl.com/y7p7w8a7>.

23. Erin Wayman, "Why Are Humans Primates?," *Smithsonian Magazine*, October 29, 2012 <tinyurl.com/y96qkqgp>.

24. Rustin Bergren, "Why can't you see electricity?" Quora.com, December 10, 2012 <quora.com/Why-cant-you-see-electricity>.

25. Rukmini Callimachi, "A Dream Ended on a Mountain Road: The Cyclists and the ISIS Militants," *New York Times*, August 7, 2018 <tinyurl.com/yd8wo5m3>.

SIMILAR TITLES BY RAY COMFORT

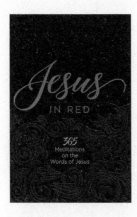

Jesus in Red: 365 Meditations on the Words of Jesus
If anything in this life deserves our undivided attention, it's the powerful words of Jesus. This inspirational daily devotional allows you to experience God's peace and presence as you reflect on the awe-inspiring teachings of Christ. Start each day off on a positive note by letting the words of Jesus speak to you and your heart.

Jesus in Red includes short meditations, soul-searching questions, and inspiring prayers.

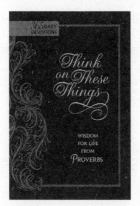

Think on These Things: Wisdom for Life from the Book of Proverbs
This 365-day devotional provides continual encouragement to live with eternity in mind. Each daily devotion includes a proverb for the day with insights, a Soul Search question to help you reflect and apply the principle personally, and a short prayer.

Grab hold of God's wisdom while cultivating a heart to reach the world with the truth of God's Word.

Available from LivingWaters.com.

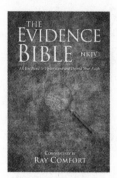

THE
EVIDENCE BIBLE

"An invaluable tool for becoming a more effective witness." —FRANKLIN GRAHAM

The Evidence Bible (NKJV) arms you not just with apologetic information to refute the arguments of skeptics, but with practical evangelism training on how to lead them to Christ.

- Discover answers to over 200 questions such as: Why is there suffering? How could a loving God send people to hell? What about those who never hear of Jesus?

- In addition to thousands of verse-related comments, over 130 informative articles will enable you to better comprehend and communicate the Christian faith.

- Over two dozen articles on evolution will thoroughly prepare you to refute the theory.

- Dozens of articles on other religions will help you understand and address the beliefs of Mormons, Hindus, Muslims, Jehovah's Witnesses, cults, and others.

- Hundreds of inspiring quotes from renowned Christian leaders and practical tips on defending your faith will greatly encourage and equip you.

The Evidence Bible provides powerful and compelling evidence that will enrich your trust in God and His Word, deepen your love for the truth, and enable you to reach those you care about with the message of eternal life.

Commended by Norman Geisler, Josh McDowell,
D. James Kennedy, Woodrow Kroll, Tim LaHaye,
Ken Ham, and many other Christian leaders.

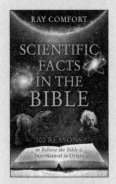
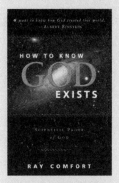

SCHOOL OF BIBLICAL EVANGELISM
Ray Comfort & Kirk Cameron

This comprehensive study offers 101 lessons on thought-provoking topics including basic Christian doctrines, cults and other religions, creation/evolution, and more. Learn how to share your faith simply, effectively, and biblically... the way Jesus did.

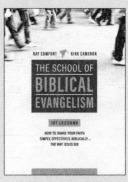

ISBN: 9780882709680

WAY OF THE MASTER STUDENT EDITION
Ray Comfort & Allen Atzbi

Youth today are being inundated with opposing messages, and desperately need to hear the truth of the gospel. How can you reach them? Sharing the good news is much easier than you think... by using some timeless principles.

ISBN: 9781610364737

BRIDGE LOGOS